Praise for S

"*Spot of Grace* is soul medicine. U⸱⸱⸱⸱⸱⸱⸱⸱⸱⸱⸱⸱⸱⸱⸱⸱⸱⸱s
to our deepest and truest selves⸱⸱⸱⸱⸱⸱⸱⸱⸱⸱⸱e
make a difference simply by being ourselves."

— M. J. Ryan, author of *Giving Thanks*

"Once again, in her own inimitable way, Dawna Markova has created a garden of earthly delights, where we can be nourished deeply. *Spot of Grace* is a treasure trove of wonders and inspiriting stories. Anyone wanting to make a difference in the world needs to read this book."

— Michael Toms, founding president of New Dimensions Media Broadcasting Network and author of *A Time for Choices*

"If you need proof that your life is a meaningful story and that you make a difference, then read this book."

— Bernie Siegel, MD, author of
365 Prescriptions for the Soul and *Love, Magic & Mudpies*

"Dawna Markova not only sees the patterns in life that connect us all in dazzling relationships; she also writes about them magically and poetically. She helps readers cultivate the ability to feel, see, and care. In a world out of balance, this capacity is more important than ever; in fact, our survival may depend on it. *Spot of Grace* is more like a revelation than a book."

— Larry Dossey, MD, author of
The Extraordinary Healing Power of Ordinary Things

"You hold a glorious, inspiriting miracle in your hand. You must read and share this treasury of redemption, compassion, and optimism. Please dip into this heart-floating stream of goodness whenever you need to remember that you do make a difference and that love really is the key."

— Jennifer Louden, author of
The Woman's Comfort Book and *The Life Organizer*

spot of grace

ALSO BY DAWNA MARKOVA

The Art of the Possible

No Enemies Within

How Your Child IS Smart
(coauthored with Anne Powell)

Learning Unlimited
(coauthored with Anne Powell)

An Unused Intelligence
(coauthored with Andy Bryner)

The Open Mind

Random Acts of Kindness
(cocreated with M. J. Ryan and Will Glennon)

Kids' Random Acts of Kindness
(cocreated with M. J. Ryan and Will Glennon)

I Will Not Die an Unlived Life

The SMART Parenting Revolution

spot of grace

Remarkable Stories of How You *Do* Make a Difference

DAWNA MARKOVA, PhD

FOREWORD BY SYLVIA BOORSTEIN, PhD

New World Library
Novato, California

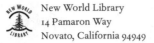

New World Library
14 Pamaron Way
Novato, California 94949

Text design by Tona Pearce Myers

Library of Congress Cataloging-in-Publication Data available.
Markova, Dawna.
Spot of grace : remarkable stories of how you do make a difference / Dawna Markova ; foreword by Sylvia Boorstein.
     p.   cm.
ISBN 978-1-57731-586-5 (pbk. : alk. paper)
1. Caring. 2. Influence (Psychology) I. Title.
BJ1475.M38 2008
205'.677—dc22   2007049251

First printing, March 2008
ISBN: 978-1-57731-586-5
Printed in the United States on 50% postconsumer-waste recycled paper

New World Library is a proud member of the Green Press Initiative.

10   9   8   7   6   5   4   3   2   1

Dedicated to the love my sister, Joan, seeded in her grandchildren:
Jordan, Max, Ashlie, Dana, Kendall

To those who came before us, who stand beside us,
and who will follow us

Each person is born with an unencumbered spot,
free of expectation and regret, free of ambition and embarrassment,
free of fear and worry; an umbilical spot of grace where
we were each first touched by God. It is this spot of grace that issues peace.

MARK NEPO, *Unlearning Back to God: Essays on Inwardness, 1985–2005*

contents

foreword

As I finished reading the manuscript for this book, I sat down at my computer, eager to write about how each of us, in addition to having our own spot of grace, functions as a communal reminder and repository of grace for everyone else. Just then, "Ding-dong! You've got mail" sounded. Because I saw that the sender was a good friend, the director of a service nonprofit organization in Los Angeles, I read the message.

She described the organization's three-day Board retreat that had just ended. Someone had been summoned away in the middle of the retreat by the news that her father was dying, and she had rushed to his bedside. Someone else had arrived grief-stricken by the news that a friend's elderly mother had been hit by a car as she crossed the street the day before and had died. Another person had hardly unpacked when urgent news from home required that she repack her bags and leave. And yet the tone of my friend's email was reassuring. She ended by saying, "I'm so glad we were all together. There was so much grief in the room, and so much loss. Everyone had something to add to the conversation — something that had just happened, or something they were reminded of. It was impossible to not notice the truth of how vulnerable to suffering we all are, all the time. And it was also clear that being with people who will hear your story and tell you their story makes suffering manageable. It renews courage."

For only the briefest of moments — because I knew some of the people in my friend's organization personally and I began to think about phoning them — I was distracted from the message I had meant to write. Then I realized that the email I had received and the one I was planning to send — and all communications, really — were the same message; there really is only one message. Life is complex and challenging and often confusing, but human beings have the unique ability to care about how they feel, about how the people who are dear to them feel, and even about how people they don't know personally feel. Hearing a story puts into motion the desire to connect.

We are empathic animals. We are moved by suffering to the desire to console, and we are also moved by beauty and marvel to the desire to celebrate. We sing along with the singing waiters who have brought a birthday cake to the table next to ours in a restaurant, knowing that whatever the birthday person's situation is, he or she has made it another year and is wishing for something good, just as we would if it were our cake. We may despair when life seems too difficult, but usually we want more of it. We hold out for the possibility of happiness. So does everyone else.

Over the years I have seen many variations of the line "Too bad life didn't come with an instruction manual." I think it *did* come with one. The instruction is, "Talk!" Tell your story. Report your experience. We encourage and console and inspire ourselves and everyone who hears us whenever we have the chance to say, "This is happening to me," or, "That happened to me." Then someone else can say or even think to themselves, "You know, when that happened to me . . . ," or, "I once knew a person who had a story like that . . . ." The stories are what convey the truth "Everything happens to everyone, some time or another." If we tell our story, and it echoes back in someone else's version, we know we are not alone. It lightens the burden when the story is difficult, and it amplifies hope when the story is — as the stories in this book are — about redemptive moments of grace.

The capacities to encourage, console, and appreciate come as standard issue of human beings, ready to be activated by real-world relationships. I love to remember that the Buddha addressed the people who sought his counsel as "O nobly born!" regardless of their social rank or life history. I think this reflected the view that the human realm, filled with the "ten thousand joys and ten thousand woes," was the most noble. It required (and allowed) human beings to look beyond themselves to the situations of everyone else — in order both to lift the heart from self-absorbed dismay and to connect it to strength.

And for me the most thrilling surprise of listening and responding — in thought or in words or deed — to someone else's story is that it redeems me from limited vision. I am continually exalted by the magic of rediscovering that in the moment I truly notice someone else's situation — when I feel another person's life and wish them well, or console them, or appreciate them — my mind unties the knots that obscure my own happiness and I am, myself, encouraged and consoled and inspired.

So get ready, as you begin this book, for your mind to fill with joy and energy and delight and inspiration. Each person's spot of grace is potentially the escape route for your mind out of its own difficulties. You will draw on the courage of others as you read their stories. You will be held up by the spirit breathed into you by the words, "I did this! I managed. I survived a very hard time. And I am left, not just managing but celebrating." What amazing grace!

SYLVIA BOORSTEIN, PHD, author of
Happiness Is an Inside Job: Practicing for a Joyful Life

spot of grace

On top of my grandmother's bureau sat a carved camphorwood box. Inside the box was a handful of dirt. When I asked her where it came from, she would say only, "Home." As far as I know, she carried the box with her for over eighty years. When she traveled in steerage from Russia and landed finally on Ellis Island, she sprinkled a pinch of the contents beneath her feet to make a friend of alien ground and bring herself home.

My life contains the seeds that have sprouted in that handful of earth. They have waited in the dark, blanketed by various hesitations. They have been watered with many tears and fertilized by the people and experiences that broke me open. May they lead us all to grow passionate minds and intelligent hearts. May they lead us out through the silence in which our wisdom is born.

garden

How Do You Call Yourself
When You Want Your Soul to Answer?

*Driven by the force of love, the fragments of the world
seek each other that the world may come into being.*

PIERRE TEILHARD DE CHARDIN, *The Phenomenon of Man*

My grandmother began to stroke my forehead very slowly, the signal that a story was on its way. Her stories always made a silken tent for the two of us to crawl into.

"Imagine, my darling, that back in the very beginning of everything, there was an immense crystal bowl floating in the dark velvet sky. Imagine it was glowing because it was made of light."

I held my breath until she continued.

"We don't know how the bowl got there or how long it stayed. But we do know that one day there was a cracking, crashing sound that was almost as big as the sky. The bowl shattered into a million, billion, trillion different seeds of light. They flew everywhere, piercing everything alive in the world. From that moment on, each living being has had, hidden in its heart, one of those tiny seeds of light."

She bent over and looked right into me with her Coca-Cola brown eyes. She whispered as if she were telling me great secrets.

"One such seed is inside of you, and one is inside of me. I call it the spot of grace. Every one of us, whether we know it or not, is supposed to find that special light. Then we are meant to grow it and shine it into the darkness of the world, helping others find their light. When everyone does, you see, the bowl will be made whole again."

"How come nobody talks about their spot of grace, Grandma?"

She leaned over and placed her lips against my ear. "Most people don't know about the bowl or that little seed of light because they don't have a grandma like you do. So when you grow up, your job will be to help them find it. Maybe you'll tell them this story. And when you do, your spot of grace will glow even brighter."

That story has carried me forward for more than six decades. It has turned every wound and tragedy of my life into a doorway. Even now, as I reach toward you, dear reader, I still think of the spot of grace as a tiny seed of light, a luminosity that results from bringing the gift that only you can bring to the rest of the human community. This gift of the soul is what lights you up and gives your life meaning. It is what helps you know who you truly are and feel as if you belong, as if you don't want to hold anything back or in. When your days are rooted in this place, you stop caring about whether you *have* enough or *are* enough. Doubt gives way to wonder. You know that you do matter, and even more, you know that the world matters to you. It is this, remarkably, that allows you to make a difference.

I have had many incarnations in this one life — teacher, psychotherapist, researcher, corporate mythologist, thinking partner, author, organizational fairy godmother. Whatever I called it, what I have been doing is supporting individuals and communities of every shape and kind in recovering their lost wisdom and liberating their full capacity. I have been learning ways to turn inward with others in wonder so they can recognize and risk growing their spot of grace. I think of it as a transformative moment of meeting, creating a "yes tunnel," where together we follow the footprints of their soul.

Something different ignites that place for each of us. My son tells me he feels grace when he jumps off a snowy cornice on skis. My nephew lights up while watching the stock market gyrate. My friend Lorin describes the feeling of union he has when singing in a church choir. I experience moments of grace when I am connecting with other people in a particular way that feels like a great melting: when I sit with someone and listen deeply to the questions his or her life is asking or when I speak to a group and feel a ribbon of stories unfolding in my mind from some source larger than myself. There is a sense in the canyons of my bones that I'm doing what I was born to do. Plato said that the greatest calling of a human being is to be a midwife to the soul of another. The Buddhists call someone who aspires to help others in this way *kalyanamitra*. John O'Donohue, Irish poet and philosopher, calls it *anam cara* — friend of the soul.

I have lived enough to realize that I can't make grace happen. But I am discovering how to create the conditions that will make it possible for it to emerge. I can't say where it comes from, but I know that it feels like a cellular sense of well-being and being well; it feels as though everything — emotion, knowledge, intellect, and intuition — comes together in a single embrace and sighs. This book is a collection of such moments.

garden

Things falling apart is a kind of testing and also a kind of healing.
We think that the point is to pass the test or to overcome the problem,
but the truth is that things don't really get solved. They come together
and they fall apart again. It's just like that. The healing comes from
letting there be room for all of this to happen: room for grief, for relief, for joy.

PEMA CHÖDRÖN, *When Things Fall Apart*

Two questions lie at the center of this book: Who helped you know
you are unique? And whose uniqueness have you recognized and
fostered?

As I write this, I've just returned from Denver, where my older
and only sister, Joan, died of a brain tumor. She was the last member
of my family of origin and one of the first people who helped me recognize my uniqueness. The world as I knew it has shattered in the
middle of my chest. During the fifteen months she was ill, I shuttled
back and forth, challenged again and again to open my heart in a very
personal hell. It was a pilgrimage of hope that has now ended. What
are the stories I can tell myself to console the orphan I have become?
What are the stories that will rearrange the pieces and make the world
whole again?

How does a hole become whole? An images arises from the
blankness in my mind. The hole becomes a void space. Avoid space.
A sterile, void space. I am closing in on myself to avoid feeling that
hollow emptiness — the feeling my sister's death has carved in my
solar plexus. Closing in the way the coffin closed on her.

Stop. I am not in the coffin. What if I open it? Open myself to the feeling, give it space. I think about the hollow space in the clay that makes a bowl possible. How can a sterile void become fertile? I think about zero. The zero that makes all numbers possible. I think about a circle, a circle that has no beginning, no end.

I walk with my questions as companions to open the space. I walk to launch them into the great vastness around me. How does "broken apart" become "broken open"? I walk to listen through the soles of my feet, to hear the stories in the earth, to reseed a larger landscape, to broaden the geography of my heart.

As I do so, my mind begins to lay down the stepping-stones of a path forward by telling me stories of how I learned to relate to sorrow in the past. A decade ago, when my father died, grief shattered my heart as it has now. I felt skinless. One dark night I wrote a poem titled "I Will Not Die an Unlived Life." It made it possible for me to breathe, and in breathing, I could float on that ocean of sorrow. Living the unlived life became the new axis of what mattered to me.

Writing that poem, and the book it grew into, opened doorways I didn't even know were shut. Much to my surprise, the poem and the book have passed from one invisible hand to another, circling the world many times. They have woven together an invisible community of people I could not have imagined existed. The emails and letters were threads across time and space. What was true for me was also true for many others. I realized that the questions that string the loom of our days and the stories that shuttle back and forth as we trudge through the events that happen to us form the fabric of life that holds us all. They can integrate fragments and moments into meaning. They can connect me with others, seen and unseen, who have the same human experience, can create a balancing structure to the isolation of despair. Diving deep enough into the darkness, I found the light of a hidden wholeness, rekindling my faith that greater forces are at work in the world than I can know. Thus I too can belong to a community, a circle — empty, fertile, and full.

As I write this, I'm one hour closer to my death than I was when I sat down at my computer. You will be one hour closer to your death when you finish reading it. I don't say this as a Zen koan or to be dramatic. Living with cancer for three decades and the deaths of my father, mother, and sister have taught me that every mindless moment is one less moment that I have to spend. No one, no matter how much they love me or how wealthy they are, can give me any more moments than the ones that exist in the diminishing space between now and my death.

When I was growing up, whenever my parents gave me a gift, they would say, "Use it well." I am acutely aware that the moments I have to live are a gift. I want to be fully alive as I spend each one. I am writing this book, therefore, as a way to make the grief I feel more comprehensible and to make what matters to me more explicit. I am writing it, dear reader, so I can profess and proclaim my faith that you too carry a seed of light, a unique prism of meaning. I offer this book as a companion while you come to recognize and grow that gift.

How Would You Live If You Knew Your Life Were an Unfinished Work of Art?

We are exploring together. We are cultivating a garden together,
backs to the sun. The question is a hoe in our hands and we are digging
beneath the hard and crusty surface to the rich humus of our lives.

PARKER PALMER, *Let Your Life Speak*

It became obvious, as I began to write this book, that if I chose to privatize my grief, I would be leaving my heart behind. Instead, I wrote with Joan floating on the surface of my mind. In this way even though she is gone, our relationship remains alive. In crafting these pages, I am bowing in respect to the love that carried us like a river — often turbulent, sometimes humble and serene — for sixty-five years.

The first time I experienced my sister's soul ignite was also the time I realized how different we were. She, age fifteen, decided to take me, eight, on a train to New York City so I could go to a museum and see real art. All she could talk about was the beauty of the paintings and sculptures in those big drafty rooms. I had never seen her so alive. At the end of the day, too exhausted to walk anymore, we collapsed on the wide granite steps in the front of the building. We sat there for an hour. I watched more people walk by than I had seen in my whole life, and never, ever, did I see two who looked the same. Each carried a unique story, an individual history and possible future. On the train ride home, all I could think about was the miracle of how each person was different from every other.

garden

11

Joan continued to love art and museums throughout her life, but her true masterpiece was her devotion to her grandchildren. I decided, therefore, to dedicate this book to the love she seeded in those five young people, to the generations that stand behind us and the generations that will follow us, and to all of us who are truly grandparents to the future.

The one quality Joan always strived to maintain was graciousness. For her, that denoted a certain public civility and elegance. I tend toward the awkward and cumbersome, but graciousness in my lexicon means a very private and spiritual sense of connection — the spot of grace.

Being the perfectly responsible older sister, she hated to be the focus of attention. She carried other people in conversation on a current of questions about what mattered most to them. As they responded with stories of their sick father or their son with autism or their last trip to Machu Picchu, she leaned in, eyes bright, lips soft. An hour could go by before she would talk about herself. This was not out of humility but rather because, for as long as I knew her, Joan just wasn't very interested in herself.

We were as opposite as two sisters could be. Questions were her native language, stories mine. If Joan paid attention to details in the outer world, I focused always on the internal horizon. If she was a genius at networking with the public, I was a shy person who flourished in solitude. We were what I call unlived parentheses of each other.

Now that she has passed, I have had to close the circle by creating dialogues between my own magnetic north and south poles. I have had to learn to ask questions of the public world and receive the stories people give me in response. I imagined creating a network of those stories and sewing them together the way Joan taught me to sew my first cotton apron.

I asked people about their spot of grace in workshops I taught, in speeches I gave, in conversations on airplanes. I sent out an email inquiry to 2,500 of Joan's friends and my own. These were the words I used:

> Settle in for a few minutes and think about a person, a group of people, an animal, or a place that helped you realize that you are unique and have something to contribute to the rest of us. Or think about someone whose spot of grace you recognized and encouraged. Then scribble it down and send it to me. It doesn't have to be correctly spelled or fancy, just authentic to you, with a few details that will bring your memories alive. You can remain anonymous if you like or use your name.

I ended it with the last lines of my poem, "I Will Not Die an Unlived Life":

> Know that in sending me your stories, you will be "risking your significance, taking what came to you as seed and passing it on as blossom, and transforming that which came as blossom into fruit."

The stories began to drift slowly into my mailboxes. At first I worried that people had no idea what I was talking about. Indeed, many people said to me, "What do you mean, 'Who taught me that I'm unique'? Unique? There are six billion people on this planet, Dawna. I'm just ordinary, normal, like everyone else." I felt great sorrow then, imagining that no one realized what a miracle their individuality really was. But after I sent out the email, thirty stories appeared one day, forty the next. Some came from people I knew, others from people I had never met. Most of them came with expressions of gratitude. "Writing this was like taking an antidepressant. I was pretty bummed out when I started, but writing it made it all come alive again."

Maybe this is why a ripple began when people who had received the email sent it to their friends. Stories came from Capetown, Auckland, Shanghai, Paducah, and Bruges. I was amazed at the responses. Each story had its own voice. Some were as simple as a South Dakota cornfield and others so complex that I had to read them out loud to understand them all the way down to the bone. How could one question evoke such a wide variety of responses? Based on past experience, I had expected to get stories primarily from women, but many men responded as well. A mother passed the invitation to her ten-year-old son. All the members of a book club in Chicago responded. Four grown siblings who are scattered across the globe each sent in a story without consulting the others, and a hospice nurse from Denver sent stories from her dying patients. Some people who I really thought would write didn't, and some people who I never thought would write anything more than a shopping list did. A few people sent in five or six stories. One woman sent in two and then changed her mind and decided to keep them private because they were so precious to her.

What was the pattern, the design, the form that was trying to emerge and reveal the meaning people had made from the question I had sent? I remember being on the deck of my cabin in Utah on a clear, velvet night, staring in awe at the splattering of light across such a vast sky. Where were the patterns? Wondering. There! The Big Dipper. There! The North Star. As I learned to recognize constellations and make up stories about them, I also recognized that they were in a slightly different place each night. Indeed, as humans had for thousands of years, I saw a great and slow turning right before my eyes. I remember thinking, "Oh, so this is how we invented the wheel!"

A question asked in wonder; a pause, a story emerges; a pause, a pattern surfaces, then meaning and form; a pause, a new possibility can be enacted. Stories are much more than entertainment. They gather our experience into shapes, taking individual moments and placing them in a cohesive movement. Each of the stories in this book was a moment, a point of light appearing in the night sky of someone's mind. Writing or telling it increased its vibrancy. If a person told as many of these stories as possible on any evening, the way the natives "talk story" in Hawaii, he or she might begin to recognize themes and patterns, a form we call purpose, meaning, direction, and movement.

What patterns did I find emerging from the widely varied stories that appeared in the darkness? For one thing, I was surprised at how many people had no idea that they were unique. For another, many people began to feel the hum and light only as a result of helping someone else recognize his or her spot of grace. In other words, doing it for someone else was generative.

Two opposite yet profound truths became evident — a balancing structure, as physicist Niels Bohr said, two banks of a river. Each story was remarkably different from all the others: a man's life was changed by the smile of a stranger thirty years earlier; a woman sat with her dying brother for days recalling the decades that had profoundly affected how she viewed the world.

On the other bank of the river were the amazing synchronicities and connections running through the stories. A woman from New Zealand wrote about learning to love more deeply than she had thought possible through tending her daughter, mute and vegetative during her last years of illness. At the same moment, on the other side of the planet, a woman in Colorado wrote of learning the same lesson while tending her friend, my sister, during those fifteen months when she was unable to speak or move. The daughter, Yarra, and my sister, Joan, died within hours of each other in June of 2007. Though they had lived thousands of miles apart, for a reason I do not know they were buried within miles of each other in Colorado. Yarra's parents found my poem in their daughter's journal and read it at the memorial service. When I received her story, I realized that I was part of an invisible community that was grieving all over the world. In that moment my tears fell into the ocean that holds us all.

We are connected in our humanity. Every other person on the earth grieves, rejoices, doubts, dies the way I or you will. At the same time, we are all remarkably different, one from the other. There isn't another one in the world like you. Two sides of a mystery, two banks of the river of life.

Another pattern that floated to the surface while reading the stories was the powerful effect that simply recognizing one's uniqueness can have on the direction one's life can take. I'm not talking about self-esteem or praise that makes you feel good for a moment. These are stories, rather, of the real power we have to influence and be influenced by each other. Again and again, the stories pointed to how one moment, one gesture or event, could illuminate the intrinsic value in a person's life and spark his or her self-worth. From then on, that person recognized that she or he belonged to the world and needed to contribute to it.

I believe it is important to read how others come to these epiphanies, when the essence or meaning of their lives appears. Such moments often cause a tiny gasp, a sacred pause in which the too-small ways we identify ourselves, the too-narrow maps we use to navigate our lives, dissolve and the landscape widens. Of course each of us must find grace in our own way, yet in exploring others' stories we may discover signposts to our own path. Perhaps the stories point to what activist Anne Herbert called "senseless gifts of beauty."

Searching for the form that would hold all the stories, I tried to sort them into baskets, like laundry — those from parents at this end, from teachers at that end, the ones about strangers in the middle. That didn't work. It felt forced, unnatural. The arc of experiences people sent me was too wide. Some people spoke directly to my question, but others seemed to be telling of luminous, transformative moments when colors were bright and their hearts carried no weight at all.

What was a form that could hold them all? What was the hidden question, eclipsed by the one I had asked, that all the stories responded to? I used this inquiry like a telescope, and then it all popped into a new focus: How does the soul expand through a life? How, as we grow up and then move forward, does that seed of light grow more vivid, manifesting through the endless choices that make up a life? I thought about what I had tagged on to the end of the invitation: "Know that in sending me your stories, you will be 'risking your significance, taking what came to you as seed and passing it on as blossom, and transforming that which came as blossom into fruit.' "

I grabbed all the stories and began sorting them again, this time into three piles: those that were about finding and recognizing the seed; those that were about using challenges to crack open the shell around the seed so it could sprout and evolve into blossom; and finally those that were about ripening into fruit and passing it on to seed the future. Seeding stories, flowering stories, fruiting stories.

I had released into a mysterious wind the precious poem that grew from grief after the loss of my father. It had blown around the world. Never had I felt so resplendently empty. The last three lines were now returning home again as the garden for this new book. A circle was being completed, the hidden wholeness emerging. Is the apple tree as amazed as I am now that the fruit released in the fall can birth an entire new orchard beneath its branches in the spring?

How Do You Make a Difference?

Strange is our situation here upon earth. Each of us comes for a short visit, not knowing why, yet seeming to divine a purpose. From the standpoint of daily life,

however, there is one thing we do know: that we are here for the sake of others . . .
above all, for those upon whose smile and well-being our own happiness depends,
and also for the countless unknown souls with whose fate we are connected
by the bond of sympathy. Many times a day I realize how much my own
inner and outer life is built upon the labors of my fellow human beings,
both living and dead, and how earnestly I must exert myself in order
to give in return as much as I have received and am still receiving.

ALBERT EINSTEIN, *Living Philosophies*

You survived as a child because others helped to maintain your life. It continues to be true today, even when you think you are abandoned, rejected, neglected, and unloved: the tomatoes you eat sustain you, the crossing guard stops the traffic so you can get to the other side of the street, the dinner offered to you on clean white plates nourishes you, the paper on which these words are printed informs you. Noticed or ignored, this web of others protects and holds you and makes it possible for you to make a difference: to take what came to you as seed and pass it on as blossom, and what came as blossom and ripen it to fruit.

Follow your own fingerprints. There they are on a child's forehead who feels safe enough to dream. And there they are on the bread that will be a young girl's breakfast. There, on the check that will pay someone's rent so his family can have safe harbor.

Often the light of this simple and profound awareness of how much you really matter to the rest of us is eclipsed as you focus attention on what is missing, the deficits, the horizons you never reach. It may seem as if everything is working against you. You may be able to think only of the mistake you made this morning, the disease that threatens you, or the words that pound against your heart in betrayal. In these moments you need to find refuge in the dark corners of your heart and solace in your own mercy. In these moments your tears can soften the tight shell that defends you. In these moments there can be a breaking apart and a breaking open so the holiness of your life can be released. These are not moments of weakness. These vulnerable, almost unbearable moments cultivate the garden in which grace can grow.

Recent findings in neuroscience teach us that our brains have the capacity to grow throughout our lives. Even after we grow up, we can grow forward. We grow through difficulties, through adversity and joy, through kindness and challenge, through beloveds and betrayers. It is our nature to grow — to become more intelligent, more fertile, wiser and more resilient.

It is all that life asks of you really: to grow what you were given, the spot of grace that is who you truly are; to allow the seeds in you to blossom in the light of the life you are experiencing; to cultivate this garden and bless the forces that have been the fertilizer, the rain, and the hoe; to open your hands and release the fruit of your existence.

You don't need money to do this. The moments you are given are your true wealth. You don't need power, influence, or fame. The sunlight brings the power; the wind carries the influence. And as for fame, well, when you allow yourself to notice all those hands that have made your growth possible, you will also recognize what you have made possible for countless others — and how famous you already are. In this very moment, one of those others may be telling a story about how you helped *them* grow forward.

What Does Your Life Most Need You to Hear?

The world changes according to the way people see it, and if you alter, even by a millimeter, the way ... people look at reality, then you can change the world.

JAMES BALDWIN, *New York Times Review of Books Interview*, 1979

More than a decade ago I felt as if the world was so out of balance that the thoughts in my brain kept rolling all to one side. Every news report I heard or read was filled with the words "random acts of violence." I read about a woman named Anne Herbert who was offering "random acts of kindness and senseless gifts of beauty."

Two colleagues, Mary Jane Ryan and Will Glennon, and I decided to publish a book with stories from people all over the country about this balancing phenomenon. I wanted to see if it was possible to instigate a worldwide shift in the way people were thinking — a small revolution, if you will. For every story of a random act of violence that was being told in the media, someone, someplace, must recount the story of a random act of kindness. That little book, like a jellyfish carried on an ocean swell, became a worldwide movement that continues to this day.

Since that time many people have asked me to create a book to follow *Random Acts of Kindness*, one that would balance the despair, darkness, and fragmentation that threaten to engulf us now. They have told me that we need stories of how each of us can and does make a difference.

Our souls are leaking and our world teeters. We are forgetting who we are and for what we have come. Our children and grandchildren are getting lost in the blur and skim of a too-shallow existence. The constant assault on our attention, from cell phones and BlackBerries, from email and instant messaging, fills any crack in our minds where light could possibly enter. We are pelted continually with someone else's images of what we should get and acquire, how we should look and who we should become, what we should think, and what meaning we should give to the events that occur. On the daily treadmill, people are just too busy to engage in reflection. Wonder is considered a waste of time or a disorder in need of medication. Attention is focused on deficits and disabilities, how and why we are pissed and disrespected. We are all gasping for air in the surge of fear that threatens to drown our dreams.

We need to remember that each of us matters. And each of us needs to remember what it is about life that matters. What has never been understood so fully before this time is that we coauthor our future. Life doesn't just happen *to* us; we inhabit a participatory universe, influencing and being deeply influenced by everything around us. The world changes as we change the stories we tell ourselves and each other about who we are and what we can make possible.

Stories stand at the foundation of memory and learning. They provide the meaning that structures our lives. Whether we tell them publicly to others or murmur them secretly to ourselves, stories fuel the engine of our desire and direct our actions. They form the strategy of our imagination, telling us, individually and collectively, who we are, what our purpose is, and how we connect, or don't, to the whole.

As soon as we join the human community, people start slipping stories into us as if they were software disks: "Oh, isn't he cute! He's colicky, isn't he? Probably has a delicate constitution just like his Uncle Sam." Or, "Everyone knows that the human race is basically hostile and aggressive. We will have war for the next fifty years." Like any great force of nature, the stories we tell ourselves and each other hold both danger and glory. Some of these myths rally against understanding; others promote it. Some are toxic and keep our problems festering; others are tonic, bringing us into healing. Some have the potential to expand possibilities; some to limit them. To live a life of our own definition, we must be able to discover which scenarios we are following and whether they help us grow the best of what we can be.

Many of us think we are too busy to open ourselves to our own souls and the gifts within. Grace requires wide moments. Creativity and innovation require a rest in the place where the music is born. And stories, well, stories want us to settle round a fireplace, stroll under some pine trees, or amble along a seashore listening to our own and each other's lives.

As you read the pages that follow, dear reader, I invite you to use the stories as mirrors to yourself. Where do you experience a resonance, a warmth, a tiny inner melting of recognition?

Pause every now and then to notice which of your own stories begin to rise to the surface of your mind. Turning toward your spot of grace in this way can have the same effect as putting a small spoonful of honey in the bottom of a cup of tea. It can, at the very least, help you remember to cherish the sweetness of life.

So often, we are, without knowing it, instrumental in a decision or a pivotal moment in another's journey. After a time of noticing these moments of grace, you may find that your life begins to have a life of its own. The people you meet, the events you experience, and the things that you do all become part of an unfolding story, one that until now you weren't aware was being told. You may find yourself trusting that, as with a seed, greater forces are at work supporting your growth. You may find that, more and more, you are glad to be alive.

We all need inspiration to reach across the abyss that divides us one from the other in this time. May this book help each of us recognize that when we risk reaching, we can and do make a remarkable difference.

seed

Who Stands Behind You?

No one has yet fully realized the wealth of sympathy,
kindness, and generosity hidden in the soul of the child.

EMMA GOLDMAN, *Living My Life*

My grandmother raised my open palm to her lips. I remember thinking that the little lines around her mouth must have been grooved in by kissing so many things. She looked into my eyes and asked in her secret, whispery voice, "Did you know that there is a river of blood that runs right beneath the surface of your skin?"

My jaw fell open like a baby bird's waiting for something delicious to drop in. I shook my head.

"Not only that, but there are so many gifts for you in that river from all those who came before you. All of their wisdom flows through the deepest part of you."

"Gifts? What kind of gifts, Grandma?"

"Oh, *ketzaleh* [little kitten], that river carries their prayers and dreams, their triumphs and grace."

She paused for several moments. My mind unfolded its wings and lifted off my bones, as I began to imagine all those ancestors wrapping wisdom and prayers in bright boxes and placing them in the fast-running river of my blood.

Then my grandmother's kisses became tiny flower petals landing on the tips of my fingers. "There is something else just as special," she continued. "No one else who has ever lived or ever will live

seed

27

has had marks like these. The prints here prove you are unique, a real miracle, one of a kind," she murmured. "They show that you carry that special light inside, that gift I've told you about called the spot of grace."

IN THE MIRROR OF HER EYES

JUNE LA POINTE • *Winchendon, Massachusetts*

My earliest memories of my grandmother, "Mamère" Mathilda, are of her hands. Oh, those beautiful, arthritic hands tipped with clear nail polish. I was amazed at what her hands could do. I stood on a chair next to her in the kitchen and watched her hands peel an apple in one long piece or roll out dough for a pie that was as thin as a sheet of fine paper. No matter what those hands were making, they'd always offer me a taste, bringing sweetness to my early childhood. Every day there was a fresh pie or cake waiting for me.

I was told she was hard of hearing from working with loud machinery in a mill, but she always heard my footsteps at night and would intercept me on my way to sneak downstairs to my parents' bedroom. I had a younger sister with a terminal illness who required extraordinary care from my mother, so Mamère filled in all the gaps for me. She invited me into her bed as a treat. And as I watched her grooming herself in the morning, she saw me and I saw her in a way no one else did. Can you understand how important that was to me?

> Every death is like the burning of a library.
>
> ALEX HALEY

I felt cherished, not forgotten, not lost in the cracks; she took time to include me in her world of daily care — for herself, for the house, for her family. I knew that I mattered to my grandmother, and so I learned to matter to myself.

seed

WHEN A RAINBOW IS ENOUGH

CONI JUDGE • *Eden, Utah*

I was a young mother of two trying desperately to cling to my career ladder with one hand and balance a baby, a toddler, and a marriage with the other. At that time I was "commuting" from Utah to California every week. I was drained and felt like I was failing everyone in my life — my husband, my children, my boss, and myself.

It was a rainy day, and I was taking the kids to the sitter before getting on yet another plane. I was driving, fighting back tears and wondering what I was doing — what I should be doing with my life and my little family.

At that moment a ray of sun came through the clouds and a rainbow appeared, framing the mountains. It was spectacular, vibrant. I turned to my two-year-old, Connor, strapped in his car seat, and said, "Look at that, Connor. It's a beautiful rainbow!"

He looked at the rainbow, looked at me, and with such seriousness said, "Mommy, God made that rainbow just for you."

A tremendous sense of comfort came over me, and his words felt true. I would find my way one step at a time, and everything would be fine and as it should be. Now, whenever I see a rainbow, I think that maybe, despite my flaws and inadequacies, I am good enough and special enough for God to sometimes make a rainbow just for me — and it took my young son's eyes to show it to me.

spot of grace

THAT SHINING

JOHN E. WELSHONS • *Little Falls, New Jersey*

One day in the 1980s, I was walking down Fifty-seventh Street in New York City, in the midst of a deep depression. I was having a difficult day, feeling troubled and anxious. Suddenly a young woman coming the other way glanced at me and smiled. Even then it wasn't common for someone to smile at a stranger in New York City, particularly a woman at a man. Her smile was just so pure, loving, and kind. It looked like a guru's smile. It magically lifted my spirits. I felt my heart open and soften. All of the problems I felt burdened with melted away.

Whether seventy or sixteen, there is in every being's heart a love of wonder; the sweet amazement at the stars and starlike things and thoughts; the undaunted challenge of events, the unfailing childlike appetite for what comes next, and the joy in the game of life.

SAMUEL ULLMAN

Now, some twenty-five years later, I still remember the beauty of her smile. I still remember the silent kindness that came from someplace shining in her, touching something shining in me. I had no idea that such a bright place existed under all that darkness in me. Knowing that changed everything. I never again have been able to take my troubles so seriously, remembering that something as simple as a smile can ignite that shining. It still amazes me that such a simple moment can have an effect that lasts for decades.

seed

I don't have kids. At least none that I know about. But twelve and a half years ago, I talked a friend into getting a puppy. I used to live around the corner from her. I said, "Get a puppy. I'll help." We went to get him, and there he was, a black, tiny, furry ball — shy and frisky. During the long drive home he fell asleep in my arms as we sang "Kookaburra Sits in the Old Gum Tree." Right then and there I could feel all four chambers of my heart expand. The puppy tumbled into my life, and I ended up coparenting him. Actually, for all intents and purposes, he became my dog. Actually, he became my son.

He's quite good-looking, and whenever people say, "Oh, he's so handsome!" I always say, "Oh, thank you." As if it had anything to do with me. I mean, really.

He's my family. My go-to guy. And when I'm feeling lost or abandoned or disappointed and I need to talk about it, we lie on the floor, nose to nose, and I pet him and cry and tell him how much I hurt. Like a baby seal, he looks at me with his dark eyes shining. And if I stop petting him, even for a moment, he squirms, as if to say, "I'm here, I'm listening, stay connected."

I forget he's a dog.

This story is about my dog, but it's about more than that. For twelve and a half years, no matter the time of day or night or the weather, I've had to take him *out* for a walk. I grew up in Skokie, in the suburbs of Chicago, where "going out" means going to the movies or the mall, so this was all new for me. I got to go outside for real. And I found out that I loved the earth! Who knew?

I remember on one of the first walks, late at night, feeling the chill on my cheeks, how I stopped, closed my eyes, leaned my head back, and thought, "So this is what the night feels like."

I didn't know that you can hear trees sighing, leaves wrinkling, petals dropping. I started to notice the moon, that faraway marble, in all its phases — sliver, shadow, or full and golden, hanging low in the sky like a translucent vanilla wafer.

And the stars — I didn't understand the stars. How they are there every night littering the sky with jewels.

I had never lain on the grass in the middle of the day to consult the clouds, breathe into them. I didn't know the sky is always changing its blue. Growing up in Skokie, I had never been on a prairie, let alone during the deep snows of winter. I had never heard the intimate sound of snow falling across an open field.

I learned that after the first fifteen or twenty minutes of walking, my body warms up and finds a rhythm. I didn't even know I had a rhythm. And the colors in the prairie, especially in the

> *Every new life is a new thing under the sun; there has never been anything just like it before, never will be again. A young man ought to get that idea about himself; he should look for the single spark of individuality that makes him different from other folks, and develop that for all he is worth. Society and schools may try to iron it out of him; their tendency is to put it all in the same mold, but I say don't let that spark be lost; it is your only real claim to importance.*
>
> HENRY FORD

seed

33

fall when the trees are naked — there are a thousand shades of green.

I never tasted rain or went out into the rain on purpose. I never noticed how everything glitters after a good rain. Every color is itself, only more so. I learned that early morning has its own smell and how tender the first signs of daylight can be.

I didn't understand any of this: sky, stars, wind, night, trees.

I didn't understand the landscape of my own life. I had no idea that this four-legged, furry creature would be the one to interrupt the loneliness that has been passed down in my family from generation to generation, that he would make me fall in love with the earth.

I will tell you this: I've traveled the world — the desert in Israel, the forest in Finland, the mountains in Oregon. And yet when I am walking in the prairie, with this black body bouncing ahead of me on the path, that is when I am most happy. And those are the moments when I know the world makes a difference to me and I make a difference to the world. Those are the moments when I find myself talking to God.

NEVER TOO WEARY

BILL KOENIG • *Seattle, Washington*

When I was in high school, my father, who was a conductor on a local freight train, would leave early in the morning. I wouldn't see him until late at night, when I would sit by him as he was changing his clothes. I can almost smell that room, as he took his overalls off and put his watch with the chain on the dresser. During that time he was there just for me. He was always so interested in hearing about me, no matter what I said. My stories seemed to mean a lot to him — any stories, really, but particularly my sports stories. They seemed to nurture and sustain him, as if they provided some kind of power in his life. What he gave me in those moments was a sense of support that's never left me. How could I not feel my spot of grace when I was received like that? To this day, so many years later, I still tell stories to anyone who listens. Maybe a too-busy father will read this and remember to give his son what my father gave me.

seed

I was twenty-eight years old, working as an editor and searching for a "real" profession. I didn't think editing was real because it wasn't creative. Writing was creative; painting was creative. One evening, at a dinner party at the home of a friend who was a painter, I went on and on about how much I envied his creativity and how I had none.

Michael took my hand and led me into another room. He proceeded to unroll about a dozen canvases, all of the same scene. "Which one is best?" he demanded. I looked them over and pointed to one. "Yes," he said. "And your ability to know that is your creativity."

His words were like the ringing of a gong. From the bottom of my soul, I got it. From that moment onward, I never denigrated my talent and have gone on to use that capacity for discernment and analysis in all the work I do. It has taken me from editing to writing and working with individuals and teams all over the world. His honoring of that which I had always taken for granted not only allowed me to claim it but also compelled me in my work to help others honor what is uniquely theirs. He and I have seen each other very little before or since. But in that moment he was an angel in my life, delivering the message I most needed to hear.

spot of grace

THE GRACE OF STRENGTH

TREY SCOTT • *Eureka, California*

Great-grandmother Peters was in her eighties, but her body was still strong and solid like the oaks outside in her yard. I could feel this strength through her nightshirt as she held me one night during a storm. We were in northern Minnesota on a feverish tour to see our relatives, most of whom lived in and around the Twin Cities. Driving through the summer Minnesota countryside, I had been struck by how green everything was. My family lived in Southern California, and I had never seen anything quite like this intense green color, nor had I ever felt the force of a midwestern thunderstorm.

I was five years old, perhaps six. We were spending the night in Great-grandma Peters's home. It seemed huge, especially with a basement and an attic full of bat droppings. Bats — cool! My parents had left us in the care of our great-grandmother, who didn't speak much English, to join other grown-ups for a night on the town. We went to bed that summer night while it was still light out. Darkness approached more in the shape of clouds than a darkening sky.

I was startled out of a deep sleep by the cracking and thundering of a storm. I thought the attic was being attacked. It was pitch-black except for blinding flashes of lightning. The world was coming to an end. I screamed and cried in terror and ran, bumping my way down the hall to my great-grandmother's door, which was open. I ran to her, and she let me hide in her nightshirt.

She gently held me close. I remember wetting her nightshirt with

seed

37

my tears. I felt her strength begin to calm my terror. I rested into her like a ship slips into a calm bay, a churning sea at its back. No words, just the sound of cracking thunder and my crying, which slowly subsided because the oak of this woman, her grace, made me feel safe in the face of the end of the world. We fell asleep in her bed, and to this day her strength is a quality I feel whenever I find myself resting up against a great oak tree.

> *Every person born in this world represents something new, something that never existed before, something original and unique.*
>
> MARTIN BUBER

How is it that time falls away so easily, dissolving like salt in warm water? No matter. Memories and feelings of grace reach across the ages to remind us that in the folds of a great oak we rest against today, are also the folds of a nightshirt wetted from tears more than forty years old. What has taken root in one act of grace is the seed of strength in me, which is both steadfast in chaos and calm in the face of fears.

ALL YOU CAN CARRY

EVE DAVIES • *Salt Lake City, Utah*

I don't remember his name, but that doesn't mean he wasn't important to me. When I was seven we moved to Dinosaur National Monument, in canyon country in Colorado. It was remote and beautiful. The nearest town, miles away, had only three hundred people, and few children lived nearby. There was no library in this part of the country. I loved the wild spaces of my 300,000-acre backyard, but I also loved books and really missed the library.

The first time I saw a bookmobile pull up right outside our house, I was ecstatic. The driver smiled when he saw the expression on my face. Eager questions bubbled out of me as I tunneled into the children's books: How often do you come? How will I know when you're coming? How many books can I borrow? He replied that he came once a month and that he would call the visitor's center, where my father worked, the day before he was going to come. I could check out four books at a time. I was crestfallen — only four? For a whole month? It seemed impossible. While I was trying to decide which of the armful to choose, his eyes twinkled. He reached for the placard with the four-book-limit notice, tipped it facedown, and said, "For you, miss, you can borrow as many as you can carry." I was so relieved.

The next month I was waiting at the edge of the road, fully prepared, when he pulled up. He laughed at the sight of me on the gravel road with an empty wheelbarrow beside me. I was so pleased with

seed

myself for coming up with such a marvelous solution, but when I saw him laugh, I was afraid that maybe this wasn't going to work. The driver, however, was delighted to see such enthusiasm. It soon became clear that we shared a love of books and stories. He started to bring me new books he thought I would like from a larger library, since I had read so many of the standard ones in the bookmobile. For three years I immersed myself in stories of faraway lands and experiences I could have only through reading. I wish I could remember his name. He watched me light up around books, and all these years later, books still connect me to my spot of grace in a very special way.

My first inkling of having a spot of grace was when I was five years old and asked my mother about my life. I was wondering why I didn't have a father.

My first few years were spent in a cradlelike security. My mother was a gypsy at heart and traveled with me and a 120-pound German shepherd named Max, who was a mangy rescue dog. He protected both of us. When I say "traveled," I mean hitchhiked. Imagine a twenty-one-year-old woman cradling an infant on her hip, a few bags at her feet and an intimidating dog at her side, standing with her thumb out on a freeway! Mom waited for a ride, and Max snapped at bumblebees. He rolled them around with his paw to stun them before swallowing.

As I got older I asked Mom, in so many words, about my story. By that time I knew about the conventional family structure and understood we did not fit in it. She explained that she had been in a relationship with my father when she was "called" to have me. She knew he did not want children and that by getting pregnant she would have to leave him. She got pregnant anyway. It was time for me to come into the world. When she announced she was pregnant, he was not happy, and she gave him an out, which he took. Mom was okay with this. It was my time.

In labor, she went into a trancelike state. She told me she was floating above her body watching herself. My spirit was with her.

She asked it my name, and it told her Isha if I was a girl and Aram if I was a boy.

Few children grow up feeling that wanted. I never felt rejected by my father but rather felt wholly embraced and loved by my mother. She told me I was unique and special and that she had freely taken risks to have me. I knew I was loved strongly for who I was. What could be better than that?

IN THE GRACE MOMENTS

SUSAN D. MARIE • *Seattle, Washington*

I came to know I was worthy of love with Grandpa Herman. He was always happy to see me. He didn't say much; he would just give me the sweetest hug. I would sit on his knee and think, "Grandpa is here, and everything will be okay." I felt safe just being. Though the visits were brief, during each one I was reminded that I was whole. Because he trusted the good in me, I could too.

Grandpa Herman once gave me a cloth tobacco pouch filled with coins. He said that each time he had thought about me, he had put a coin in the pouch. Before that, I didn't know that people thought about me even when I wasn't with them.

> *Find the seed at the bottom of your heart and bring forth a flower.*
>
> SHIGENORI KAMEOKA

When my Grandpa Herman passed on, I was five years old. Unlike my cousins, I was allowed to go to his funeral. I remember thinking, "That's not my grandpa in that casket. My grandpa is right here, behind everyone, watching all of us, and that is a good thing." That night a presence came to visit me. I knew it was my grandpa watching over me and helping me in all that was to come.

Now I help other people recognize that they are whole, that they are enough, and that they can listen to their own inner voice for guidance. I am really just giving them what he gave to me.

seed

A HAWK'S JOURNEY

DALE BRYNER • *Ithaca, New York*

Nine years ago I needed guidance to make some important decisions. I formulated my questions and went to the land to sit for forty-eight hours, inspired by native vision quests. I found the clarity and support I sought, and after two days and nights I left the beautiful woodland spot. However, on my quest I had completely forgotten one question: why am I slow in learning? As a young girl in public school I had often felt that my learning style didn't fit the norm. More recently I saw that important teachings had come to me only in adulthood. Why hadn't they come earlier?

Seven weeks after my quest, on a November afternoon, Spirit answered this unasked question eloquently. I stood in a prairie meadow behind my home. A large kettle of hawks came flying from the eastern horizon over my head toward the west. I called to them, wishing them well on their migrating journey, and marveled at the synchronized beauty of their flight. A few minutes later, several more groups followed, flying directly overhead. It was a marvelous sight!

After they passed, I stood there and watched a single dot emerge from the eastern horizon and fly slowly and steadily toward me. It was one lone hawk, lagging behind the others. I called to it passionately, cheering it on. After it passed, I realized that even though it seemed alone at this moment, it was being called by the same inner direction as the hawks in front of it. I trusted it would remain true to its course and arrive at its destination with the others.

Shortly after, I returned to the house, but something pulled me back out. As I looked east again, I saw more kettles appearing over the horizon. They continued to fly overhead for twenty minutes, and I was in awe at their numbers. My perspective of a "slow" one was put to rest. I saw that all the birds were following the same inner guidance. They were all going home. They said to me, "You are not slow. You are where you are supposed to be, behind some and before others. Carry your truth and know we are all connected and vital in this seamless journey home." In that moment of grace, I realized I had been following my path all along at a rhythm that was uniquely my own.

seed

THE PASSIONATE PILOT

MICHELLE ZOU • *Redmond, Washington*

I began to recognize my son's spot of grace the moment I saw his passion for flying. He's only three. Where did it come from?

I first saw it when I took Andrew to China to visit his grandparents when he was two. He spent many hours looking out the airplane windows to see the clouds, the ocean, the mountains, and the houses on the earth. He was fascinated by the plane's takeoff, high flying, and landing at the airport. He loved the experience! From then on, whenever there was a plane flying in the sky, he would spot it, no matter how far away. After we returned from our trip to China, he insisted I take him every weekend to the Museum of Flight in Seattle. When I tired of doing that, we agreed we would go once a month. He uses his little arms to simulate how a plane takes off, climbs up, and lands on the ground. He builds planes with LEGOs, flies planes made of paper, and draws planes on the wall. In his room, there are planes everywhere. Andrew has even made up songs about them: "A plane is flying in the sky. . . ."

Of course, Andrew says that when he grows up he wants to be a pilot. I know he's only three, but somehow I believe him. When he points excitedly with his little fingers at the plane flying in the sky, I am so touched by the passion from this precious heart. What could be more beautiful than a young boy experiencing such joy? Where does it come from? I will do whatever I can to encourage him to follow his dream fully. We all deserve that.

SAVING GRACES

JENNY ESSENCOURT • *Cambridge, Massachusetts*

When I was seven, my saving graces helped preserve my spot of grace. I had a dog, a black Lab mongrel, whom I named Benjamin K. Finkelstein (because I thought that was the cutest name I'd ever heard), and a Persian tabby cat known as Mr. Tibbetts. I lived outdoors a lot because there was trouble in my family, and I wasn't safe inside. Benjy and Mr. T went with me everywhere. We walked for miles, all over the woods and beyond. I knew that they totally loved me and would keep me safe as well as they could. They also knew that I totally loved them.

> *Before you tell your life what you intend to do with it, listen for what it intends to do with you. Before you tell your life what truths and values you have decided to live up to, let your life tell you what truths you embody, what values you represent.*
>
> PARKER PALMER

We talked all the time. We went out in a rowboat on the little pond at the bottom of the hill, and Mr. T sat in the bow grooming himself while Benjy sat in the stern watching his reflection and drooling on the frogs and turtles passing below us. We noodled around the pond, exploring and having adventures, as I rowed for hours in a safe universe. When I was with them, life was perfect. I knew without a doubt that I was whole and unique.

seed

HOW COULD ANYONE EVER TELL ME

LAURA L. THEIMER • *Flagstaff, Arizona*

Near the end of my forty-ninth year, I attended a retreat focused on care for those whose lives had been touched by HIV/AIDS. One of the exercises had us sitting in a large circle on the floor listening to the song "How Could Anyone Ever Tell You You Are Anything Less Than Beautiful?" by Libby Roderick. We had been instructed to listen to the words deeply as we slowly looked around the circle, being sure to stop for a moment to gaze into each person's eyes.

A woman I didn't know whose nametag said BEA sat across the large circle from me. When I reached her face, something in the dancing sparkle of light shining through her blue eyes whispered to my soul, "Rest here a moment." I let my eyes get soft while I held her gaze for what must have been just a few seconds but felt like a spacious eternity. Soft tears began to roll down my cheeks as I saw myself reflected in her eyes, and I knew she was seeing beneath the surface to the beauty of who I really was.

I still can't explain what happened or why. I'm not even sure that matters. What does matter is that to this day, whenever I feel lost, I play that song and I'm transported back to that moment when the holiness of myself was seen and released.

THE CEO'S DAUGHTER

DAWNA MARKOVA

I never heard my father say, "I love you." He said many things to me in his lifetime, but never that. My mother collected newspaper clippings that chronicled his journey from inner city street fighter to CEO of a major Chicago corporation. He often said he regretted never having a son, an heir to whom he could pass on the legacy of knowledge gathered as he climbed to the top of the corporate ladder.

He lacked one thing, however, and it was his greatest secret and most profound shame. I remember going to his huge office every day after school. My feet left prints in the plush burgundy carpeting as I approached the immense mahogany desk. I pulled myself up onto the tan leather swivel chair. The only things on the shining desktop were a large reel-to-reel tape recorder and a very thick pile of papers held in place by a crystal weight carved with the company insignia.

Day after day, I pushed the button on the tape recorder and began to read the papers, one by one, into the microphone. Then, when I had finished, I'd slip my hand under the big black and green blotter and find the quarter my father had left me so I could buy a hot fudge sundae on the way home. No one ever found out about this ritual. It was our secret. No one ever found out he couldn't read a word.

When he returned home from work every day, he would slip on a pair of steel-rimmed glasses and sit in a big brown wing chair with a newspaper spread wide between his hands. He moved his head back and forth in the motion people often use while reading. I'd slip under the paper and crawl up on his knee to ask my inevitable question, "Daddy, do you love me?" He'd ruffle my hair, reach in his pocket, and whisper in my ear, "Here's a nickel; don't tell your mother."

When I was a teenager, I used to wear his huge white starched shirts to school over jeans, the sleeves rolled up, my hair in a ponytail. The bigness and stiffness never bothered me. I felt protected, surrounded in his certainty. But still I yearned to hear those words he'd never say. The nickel became a quarter, then a dollar. After college, I stopped asking. I went into therapy, pounded on a pillow with a tennis racket, and shouted, "I hate you, I hate you, Daddy! Why won't you ever tell me you love me?" When I was fully grown, with a child of my own, he was saying, "Here's five dollars; don't tell your mother."

> There is in each of us an ongoing story. It contains our meaning and our destiny. . . . This is our "soul story.". . . And our deepest meaning is to stay with that story.
>
> AL KREINHEDER

During the last years of his life he had Alzheimer's disease. That lion of a corporate commander sat shrunken and unshaven in a black rocking chair in Hollywood, Florida, staring into worlds I couldn't see. I don't know if he could have responded if he'd wanted to, but for two years there was nothing. On what turned out to be my last visit to him, I knelt down on the floor and took his face between my hands. More than anything, I wanted him to know, to receive, all that I felt for him. I whispered fervently, "I love you, Daddy." His watery blue eyes reflected nothing. He was locked behind walls I could not climb.

I got to my feet, slipped my purse over my shoulder, and turned away, about to leave, when a thought crossed my mind. I reached into my wallet, pulled out a five-dollar bill, put it in his limp hand, and murmured in his ear, "Here's five dollars; don't tell Mom." Immediately he blinked, looked up at me, and smiled as he said in a gentle voice, "I love you too, sweetheart."

Those were the last words I ever heard him speak. He returned to the place behind the walls, and I went home. Still, in that one moment of grace, the best in each of us reached out and found the other.

seed

HEART-FILLED HANDS

JACQUELINE DEBETS • *Arcata, California*

My grandmother Ruth had a spot of grace, and she recognized mine as well. You wouldn't see hers in anything external — not in the clothes she wore or the fancy things she owned. It was just in how she glowed in the world.

I took care of her in the last years of her life. She was incontinent, and I cleaned her. She never lost her dignity and always thanked me. One time my mother was frantically trying to clean up, and Grandma Ruth looked exhausted. I offered to help. Grandma looked at me glowing and said, "No one can do it like you do. Your heart is in your hands." I have never forgotten that message, and I try to live it daily as a way of appreciating her.

ONLY THE TRUEST OF LOVES

ZERELINA MUKHERJEE • *Redmond, Washington*

It was May 10, 2003, around three in the afternoon. My back was aching, and I was tired and in no mood to celebrate my birthday. I was also five months pregnant with my first child. My husband and I work at the same company, so I wasn't surprised when he dropped by, but it was too early for him to be leaving work. He asked me to step out of my office. I turned the corner, and there were my mom and dad, who had flown across the country from Florida to Washington to be with me on my birthday. Even though I was going to be a mother, that was exactly what I needed — my mom.

I'm the support for my family, the strong one, the one who can deal with anything, the one everyone turns to with their problems, the one who makes plans and takes action. But at that moment, I burst into tears of joy that I could not contain. My heart was spilling over. My husband had seen deep into me, down to a secret soft spot that only the truest love could find. If he could find it, I knew it must be there. Even very strong people can have tender hearts that need to be known.

seed

A BLUEBIRD NAMED Z

PERIS GUMZ • *Belmont, Massachusetts*

My mom was a queen of grace. Her name was Zora. For many, many years she wore the letter Z stitched on the left shoulder of all of her clothes. The letters were pre-embroidered, purchased in all colors, and she sewed them on herself. It was only one of her trademarks. She was also a fabulous dresser, had many pairs of glasses to coordinate with her outfits, and always smelled of carnations. She loved the sun, Croatian tamburitza music, singing, dancing, and, more than anything, her family.

She guided me with stories, and I grew up feeling like a cross between a Balkan peasant and the Little Engine That Could. She told me funny and poignant stories about our family, so I understood the quirky, resourceful, and good-hearted lineage I was part of. She also told me stories about myself, things I did when I was younger that simultaneously evoked and confirmed my gifts. When I was three, she said, I'd let go of her hand to sit with old, unshaven men on park benches — the ones most people would avoid — and ask them, "Do you know my poppy? His name is Eli Peris." I grew up knowing that I could talk to everyone.

My mom asked me each day, "Who is the prettiest girl in your school?" I always answered, "I am, Mommy." To which she'd reply, "Who is the smartest kid in your school?" To which I would again reply, "I am, Mommy." We would conclude this litany with one more question: "And who has the nicest clothes of everyone in your school?" Without hesitating, I'd reply, "I do, Mommy."

My mother gave me so much guidance, and mostly it was fun. I didn't especially like hearing, "Into each life some rain must fall," but that too has turned out to be worthy wisdom. She was always ready to enjoy me. When I burped loudly, she'd say, "Doesn't she burp well!" and we'd both laugh. With that kind of encouragement, who wouldn't take chances?

> The great problem facing us is that the means by which we live have outdistanced the spiritual ends for which we live. . . . The real problem is that through our scientific genius we've made of the world a neighborhood, but through our moral and spiritual genius, we've failed to make it a brotherhood.
>
> MARTIN LUTHER KING, JR.

My mom passed seven years ago, with my sister and me at her side, all of us letting go together. It was one more gift from her, one more moment of grace. I feel her love every day, sometimes like a bluebird on my shoulder. Sometimes like the letter Z.

seed

HARMONY WHEREVER HE GOES

ANONYMOUS • *Boulder, Colorado*

I ran away from home as a young teenager and grew up on the streets of a city with very little nurturing, so my awareness of my spot of grace formed like a mosaic of many moments. But I recognized my husband's immediately.

When I first met him, I felt that his heart beamed out of his hands and eyes and he was a warm glow-ball of unconditional love. I was right. Even after the years we've been together, it shines on and on. He has a great sense of humor and the hands of a healer. He has the uncanny ability to find creative and inventive solutions to a variety of physical, electrical, and mechanical problems. What's more, he is able to see things impersonally, and whenever I talk to him about a difficult situation with another person, he somehow manages to point me toward peace — toward seeing what all of us have in common. This used to be frustrating for me, as I wanted him to see how right I was. Now I know him to be one of my greatest teachers. He is a man who has figured out how to be both strong and kind, loving his children and holding them with unwavering commitment.

My husband makes harmony wherever he goes, whether through music, with people, or with touch. I know that all the discord of my early years has made me grateful for every day I have the privilege to know him.

SUNSHINE IN ITALY

STEPHANIE CRAIG • *Loveland, Ohio*

About six years ago I was on a business trip to Pescara, Italy. One evening after work I decided to visit one of the boutiques near my hotel. In true Italian style, the owner guided me through her store and, despite the language barrier, tried to help me find what I needed. As I made my purchase, she looked intently into my eyes, pointed outside at the sky, cupped her hands around my face, and said something in Italian that I interpreted as, "Your face looks like the sun." With my curly blond hair, light complexion, and rounded face, I thought she was pointing out the obvious. I guessed Italians didn't see blondes up close very often. I smiled, nodded, thanked her, and was on my way.

The next day I found myself back in her shop, this time with my dear Italian friend, Rosa. The store owner recognized me immediately and pulled Rosa aside to tell her in their language what she had told me the day before. Rosa came back to me with a stunned look and said, "This woman knows you very well, Stephanie. She says the light of the sun shines from within you."

Since that day I think of those words every time I look at myself in the mirror, and it makes me smile. A woman who crossed my life in an instant gave me the gift of a lifetime. She showed me my soul, my gift to share with the world. Sunshine.

seed

BEA MAH HOLLAND, EDD • *Lexington, Massachusetts*
with LOU ANN DALY, MARGARET LEDGER,
KELLIE WARDMAN O'REILLY, *and* KATHLEEN ALFIERO

Since 1994 — year in and year out — a group of us has been meeting every six weeks to serve as midwives to each other's dreams. The shape of the group has changed over time as women left, moved away, passed away, or joined. For the past ten years the Wise Women's Group has consisted of the same five members. We are from a wide variety of educational and professional backgrounds. Some of us are youngsters, including Kellie, who started with us when she was twenty-six, and we range to age sixty-four. We come from several different heritages, including two of us who were born outside the United States.

We began with the lofty goal of wanting to appreciate people, their motivations, and their behavior in new ways, but we have long since morphed into an intimate community where there are no holds barred regarding topic or expression. There have been work transitions for every one of us, a marriage, a divorce, a baby, a new tea shop, children leaving home, publications, and death. We are a safe, honest, loving circle where we care deeply about each other and remind each other to care for ourselves. Indeed, we tough-love each other, inviting, nudging, pushing each other to break barriers and to be our brilliant, gorgeous, talented, fabulous selves.

We journey from three New England states, gather at an accessible restaurant at 4:30 PM and adjourn by 9:00 PM. Each of us in turn gives an update of what has been happening in her life, and others ask clarifying questions, paraphrase, or connect the update to past themes raised by the focal person. We are often led to explore emerging themes that reveal individual, collective, and sometimes universal insights about using our gifts in the world.

> *Stories are our nearest and dearest way of understanding our lives and finding our way onward.*
>
> URSULA LE GUIN

We have become powerful catalysts in each other's lives. Lou Ann has given birth to a potent book titled *Humans Being*. Marg continues to shape hospice, as demonstrated in her book, *Leaving This Life with Hospice: Stories of Wonder and Hope*. Kathleen has manifested much brilliance in education circles through her Celebrate School People initiative. Kellie has completed her master's and is now pursuing a lifelong dream of teaching and writing. I have learned to appreciate my unique gifts, such as my calm and my ability to pose questions that tap into individuals' and teams' most elemental yearnings. I can't imagine a richer spot of grace than our Wise Women's Group.

seed

BEYOND THE EXPECTED

MARY BRASS • *Lennox, South Dakota*

I was twelve years old when the gentleman from the city offices stopped in our driveway looking for my father. He wanted to see the building permit for the shed Dad was constructing in our backyard. I was intimidated by the thought of visiting with this city official, but Dad was out of town, Mom was running errands, and I was the oldest child home at the moment, so there was no one else to send him to for answers. Did Dad have the required permit? I answered his questions as truthfully as I could, and soon the man departed with the request that Dad give him a call.

When my father returned I told him about the incident and relayed the message to please call, which he did. I had fulfilled my responsibility to the city official and was happy to be done with my part in the matter. But Dad made a point of telling me that when he called him, Mr. City Official told him that I was a very poised young lady. I was so flattered — by the compliment from the stranger and, even more, that Dad thought it important to tell me. It is surprising to me that more than four decades later I look back on that event as having a significant effect on my life. It was the earliest inkling I had that I was capable beyond my own expectations.

spot of grace

GAIL VAN KLEECK • *Westwood, Massachusetts*

There were five children in my family. I was the oldest; my brother, Bruce, was the youngest; and we had three sisters in between. Wanting to support us to become all that we could be, our mother began looking for our strengths and gifts when we were very young. Bruce could build anything. Our mother encouraged his gift with tools, books on architecture, and trips to see unusual buildings. Christine was musical and artistic, so our mother found teachers to develop those gifts. Mary loved to care for and bandage her dolls, and our mother encouraged her commitment to others. Lesley, who was drawn to nature, was also artistically talented. Our mother encouraged her as well.

I, by contrast, was painfully shy, desperately wanting to blend into my peer group and shunning anything that would make me stand out. Our mother, however, thought I had a gift for writing and found me pretty notebooks in which to put my words. When I was about ten she noticed I liked helping rearrange furniture, and she assigned a bookcase to me. I loved having the responsibility for that bookcase. I moved its contents around for years, completely redecorating it for every conceivable holiday.

At the same time, Mom kept encouraging me to write. She called when I was in college. "Are you writing?"

"No, Mom, I'm too busy with school."

"You need to keep writing, dear."

seed

61

She called when I had a family of my own. "Are you writing, dear?"

"No, Mom, I'm too busy with the kids."

"You need to keep writing."

Sometimes, after hanging up the phone, I'd notice another of life's simple lessons that I felt compelled to record. She asked me the same question when I was discouraged about finding a publisher for my first book. She asked it again after my second book came out, when I thought there was nothing more for me to say. "You need to keep writing, dear. You need to keep using your gifts."

> *Only by recognizing greatness in others will you manifest greatness in your own life. You cannot become something you cannot perceive.*
>
> MORRIS WALKER

My mother died several years ago. The bookcase she once assigned me grew into an interior design business that has given me both pleasure and a livelihood for more than thirty years. I write a regular column titled "Simple Wisdom," which helps people see the world differently. It keeps me from taking life for granted. It causes me to feel gratitude, wonder, and occasional outrage more poignantly. It makes me know that one of the most important things we can do with our lives is to seek what is good and growing and possible in others.

There are times when each of us simply needs someone to believe in us until we find enough courage to believe in ourselves. Yes, Mom, I am writing.

Grandma Clara died before my mother was married. I never met her, yet I know that she loved me. I walked around holding her hand (though no one else could see it) and talking to her (though no one else could hear). Whenever I needed her, she was always there. My uncle Boris was the one who taught me that people could still love you even if they were dead. He died when I was two, but in those two years, Uncle Boris looked at me and held me in such a way that I just knew I mattered in this world. I didn't have words, but I had an experience that taught me all I needed to know.

Our next-door neighbor, a few years later, was a middle-aged Italian man who worked on the outside of his house in the summer with no shirt on. He had big muscles and tattoos and stubble on his face. He called me his little Prima Donna when I danced and spun on the lawn. I felt again that feeling I had with Uncle Boris, and I knew I was beautiful in a one-of-a-kind way. My parents were scared for some reason and told me I could never talk to him again, but I walked around holding Grandma Clara's hand and feeling Uncle Boris and him whenever I needed to feel like a beautiful prima donna. I still do!

seed

THE HIDDEN MAGNIFICENCE

KATHY CORDOVA • *Pleasanton, California*

I always figured I was smart, but I never saw this as a big advantage. If anything, being "the Brain" had a negative connotation in the time and place I grew up in. I loved to curl up with books — even an ancient collection of the *World Book Encyclopedia*, given to me by a great-aunt — while everyone else on my block was outside playing kickball. I was different, the bookworm, and that was not a good thing.

I always got top grades in school without working too hard. I glided along, taking my natural gifts for granted and even downplaying them so that I wouldn't stand out too much.

Then came fifth grade. I had the terrible luck of being assigned to the class of the most feared and hated teacher in the whole school, Mrs. Claggett. She seemed about a hundred years old and had quite a reputation. "Claggett/Baggit" was the secret nickname whispered all over the school.

Mrs. Claggett never smiled, never laughed or made jokes, and regularly engaged in the kind of ruthless humiliation of her students that would probably get her fired today. I kept my head down and my pencil up and tried my best not to attract attention. Then came the big culmination of fifth grade, our "States Book," in which we had to report in detail on every one of the fifty states, draw colorful maps of their topography, report on their products and population, and record lots of other senseless details that I have long since forgotten. I worked really hard on it and expected a good grade. But when the projects were returned to us, I discovered that I got a C-minus, the worst grade I had ever received in an academic subject.

We all had to have personal conferences with the teacher about the projects. When it was time for me to meet with Mrs. Claggett, I was almost in tears. I was so scared of what she would say about my book. I wish I'd had the wisdom to keep a journal back then. I can't remember her exact words, but I will never forget the significance of what she told me that day. The message was that I was smarter than this effort, that I could do better and must try harder. And then she said one thing that I remember clearly. She said that I was so smart that she could even see me going on to get a PhD! It was almost as if she was demanding that I bring forth some magnificence that she knew was hidden inside me.

> *The more light you allow within you, the brighter the world you live in will be.*
>
> SHAKTI GAWAIN

It's hard to describe the impact her words had on me. Nobody in my family had ever gone beyond high school. We never talked about college, and I hadn't even considered it until that moment. I can't remember if I even knew what a PhD was (I think she had to explain it to me), but I knew in that moment I had something greater inside of me than what had been expected up until that point.

For years, despite having no role models and no money, I had the resolute goal of getting a PhD. That vision propelled me through four years and a bachelor's degree at a wonderful university. I took a couple years off from school to pay off my student loans. That time turned into a couple of decades of working, getting married, and

seed

having kids, but I continue to think of that PhD, and I may still get it someday. The phrase that comes to mind for me is, "Aim for the stars, and you will reach the moon." Mrs. Claggett's belief in me was a finger pointing to the moon, a catalyst for a journey that has led to places that I would have never dared to dream of on my own.

MARCELLA BAKUR WEINER, PHD • *Brooklyn, New York*

When I was a child, I had a routine tonsillectomy. My parents took me home, caring and loving as always, but within a week I was swollen head to toe. Frantic, they rushed me to a nearby hospital. This was before antibiotics were in common use. As a result of the carelessness of someone during that routine operation, I had blood poisoning. The story from there on is fuzzy in my memory, but I know I had numerous transfusions.

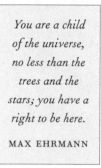

You are a child of the universe, no less than the trees and the stars; you have a right to be here.

MAX EHRMANN

My mother told me repeatedly, with joy in her sparkling blue eyes, "This man, this man I never knew, gave blood to you over and over again. If only I knew who he was, I would give him the largest reward but most of all my deepest gratitude for saving my youngest daughter's life. But since I can't, I pray for him. I pray for God to find him and reward him somehow."

The doctors did not think I would survive the blood poisoning, but I did, in part because of the attention of my mother. Because of the illness, I almost never went to school. I read voraciously. My mother played with me and shared her stories of Russian life with me, telling me stories every day that were better than Tolstoy's.

When I did finally go to school, I found it immensely boring. I longed to go back home, to hear my mother's lessons for the day and play with the dolls she made me from dish towels.

seed

I was deeply attached to her. She was beautiful to look at, an outer mirror for her inner self. Being with her transformed me. No school could compete. The deluge of pure facts at school couldn't compare with the delights of life she showed me with such enthusiasm, a panorama of God's offerings for us to enjoy. In her exquisite care, I came to realize that I must be worthy of such love and likewise that I must be able to give such love.

My great-grandmother passed away long before I was born, but I feel she is part of who I am today. The kindness and strength my mother learned from her were passed on to me. Through the stories my mom has shared about my great-grandmother — the love they had for each other and the life lessons my mom learned — I've come to know my great-grandmother and her grace.

What she taught my mom was not how to have the best life in a materialistic way but rather the importance of a good heart and empathy to feel how others are feeling. It was my great-grandmother who saw the spot of grace in my mother and encouraged her in ever so loving a way to be the best person she could be despite life's challenges.

These values were then reflected in the way my mom raised me. When I was growing up, she often would say, "If your great-grandmother were alive today, she would be so proud of and adore you."

My mom grew up in a small village in Korea, where girls were not encouraged to get a higher education but instead were responsible for taking care of the farm and house. I believe if she had had the opportunities and resources I have had, she would have become a great doctor or a teacher, touching many people's lives in a meaningful way. Because of this, I often feel my success is my mother's success. After all, it was her personal sacrifice that got me to the States and to where I am today.

seed

69

I feel fortunate to be part of this family lineage of strong women. Moving forward in life, I do not think only of myself and my own success; I carry the hopes my mom has for me and the grace and well wishes from my great-grandmother.

When I was six, my older cousin Beth brought her boyfriend home from university for a school break. They were "serious," as we said then, which meant engaged. I was enthralled with Beth. She was the most glamorous and charismatic person in my world, mesmerizing and funny. I adored her to the point of worship! She included me in her activities with "the boyfriend": skating at the local rink, trips downtown, movies, dinners out. I was thrilled beyond words.

What sticks out most about their visit, however, is that Beth insisted her fiancé play games like Concentration and Yahtzee with me, telling him I was some sort of child prodigy. She told me that I was clearly the smartest person in the family and that I was going to do great things with my life because I was so talented. Well, I thought, if this marvelous, amazing creature sees unique value in me, she must be right.

From that day forward, I truly believed I was smart. I never questioned it. I was convinced I could do anything I wanted. It didn't matter that I wasn't good at math because I kicked butt in foreign languages, geography, history, and English. Outside the classroom, the belief that I was unique gave me the confidence to carry myself with positive energy and meet new people with great enthusiasm. I believed in myself because somebody accomplished and special believed in me.

It never occurred to me until I took the SATs in my final year of

seed

high school that I was anything less than intelligent. A fairly low score dented my confidence for some time, but I eventually navigated my way. I am now in my late thirties, and being the smartest person alive is far less important to me than being uniquely who I am. And Cousin Beth is coming to visit next week!

FEISTY

BETH BLACK • *Orlando, Florida*

As my daughter grew up, she had one special friend from fifth grade through high school. Nicole was a petite, scrappy girl who rarely smiled and harbored a chip on her shoulder. She grew up without a father, and her mother was disabled. While love surrounded her in her family, she shouldered a great deal of responsibility and always seemed resentful and embarrassed by her life circumstances. She frequently came to our house after school, and one day I asked the girls about their dreams for the future. Nicole wanted to be a designer but dismissed the dream as impossible because of financial limitations and general hopelessness. Over the years, I told her what I saw in her — a strong, feisty, bright girl who could become anything she was willing to put her mind to. I knew this was true. I knew that she was a fighter and resourceful.

> *The shortest distance between the truth and a human being is a story.*
>
> ANTHONY DE MELLO

Years later, Nicole, now a designer, told me that my belief in her and my words of encouragement gave her the confidence to go to school and pursue her dream. I was surprised and touched. Kind words really can be taken to heart to fuel the inner fire. How amazing it was to hear from Nicole, after all those years, that the simple act of reflecting back the light and beauty I saw in her had the power to transform her life! That power is within the reach of all of us.

seed

THE WOMAN AT THE WINDOW

DEANNA "DEE" MCLAUGHLIN • *Salt Lake City, Utah*

For many years, my mother was not very present in my life or even interested in me. But during the last couple years of her life, I began to recognize something in her I had never known before. She spent most of that time looking out the window of her apartment, watching the world, I suppose. She knew when everybody in the neighborhood came and went. She made up stories about their lives. Some stories were rooted in what she knew about them, but some she created. She would tell them to me, and then, like a spool of thread unraveling, other stories would emerge about her own life and history.

She talked about her childhood, growing up poor on a strawberry farm, and how much she hated strawberries now because of how many she had picked then. She told stories about being the youngest of nine children and how lonely she was because her oldest brothers and sisters were gone and married with children when she was born. She spoke about her father and how he had not allowed her to go to nursing school but insisted she go to secretarial school, even though she had saved the tuition money herself. And she told stories about how much she loved her mom and how good her mom had been to her, protecting her from a father who could be aloof at best and physically cruel at worst.

> *The range of what we think and do is limited by what we fail to notice.*
>
> R.D. LAING

For forty-odd years, I had known almost nothing about who my

spot of grace

mother was as a person. Now she was becoming real to me. Suddenly I wanted to spend time with this woman I had avoided for so long, so I could get to know her even better. She spoke as if in a trance. I think she knew I was there, but that wasn't what mattered. It was her life unfolding in these fascinating stories that mattered. It was true that she was in an old body that wasn't working very well, but I no longer saw her in the old way as "mother." She became a whole woman whose life had made a difference. Through the stories she told, a window in my heart had opened, allowing me to feel great compassion and see her spot of grace.

Who helped me see my spot of grace? I'm frozen somehow by this question. Throughout my life, I've often chosen to go it alone. I'm an "I don't need help . . . I don't need you . . . I can prove it myself" sort of guy. Underneath that "me" hides a shrouded fear: that I am somehow not worthy enough to believe in myself, to deserve help, to feel joy deeply, to fulfill my calling. On the outside I've often related normally to people while inside feeling scared and withdrawn. To acknowledge someone for helping me know that I had something unique, something special to give the world, really shatters this belief that I can do everything alone.

When I start pulling on the thread of this question, my thought jumps to something easy, current, tangible. Two years ago I was a new triathlete, doing the "I don't need help" routine. A local running-store owner and friend, Mark, welcomed me to cycle with him and his training buddies. He was a veteran Ironman triathlete, and I was honored to be invited out for their Sunday morning rides. After my first ride, he invited me again. To someone who had always been picked last for playground sports — any sport, for that matter — this was incredibly flattering.

Each week Mark rode next to me for long stretches, chatting about life. Then he said, "Come on a long ride with us. It's only thirty miles. You're strong enough, Patrick. You ride well." I acted as if the feedback didn't matter, but the following week I went along for the ride. I somehow believed him, trusted him, even though I didn't believe that I could make it.

Slowly but surely, my belief in myself started to catch up to Mark's. Today, after a lifetime of inactivity and no sports accomplishments, I have four triathlon seasons behind me, and I'm training for my first Ironman. What's amazing to me is that I truly believe, with every cell of my body, that I will succeed and safely swim 2.5 miles, bike 112 miles, and run 26.2 miles. I'm still blown away by the profound impact Mark's belief in me had on my physical abilities.

I pull further on the thread. This one example opened my eyes fully to the sheer number of people who have been accompanying me all along my journey, some carrying me forward on their shoulders, some cheering me on from the sidelines. At various moments over the past five years, my friends have stirred my desire to chase my career dreams. Gifted health practitioners have believed in my being whole and complete. Most profoundly, though, I notice how my soul mate of twenty years has been standing by and cheering for me all along. She not only saw that spot of grace inside me but also believed in every dream I had, including the unspoken ones only my soul knew existed.

Sometimes it's the simple, obvious things like this triathlon experience that cause us to see life more clearly. As I write this, I feel such gratitude for all those who see my spirit and reflect my potential back to me, waiting for me (once again) to catch up with them.

seed

A WEB OF GRACE

MARY GELINAS • *Trinidad, California*
with KAREN BUCKLEY, MARY CURRAN (1931–2002), CATHY DEFOREST,
BRENDA DONAHOE, *and* MARION VITTITOW

The five of us met for the last time on a foggy San Francisco Bay morning last May. We huddled in the small living room of a friend's apartment. We began this circle twenty-one years ago to help me recover from a disabling neck injury. One of the hardest things I ever had to do was ask my busy friends to gather every week to support my healing, but it was slightly less onerous than surgery.

We met for a year, beginning by creating a medicine wheel of rocks, candles, ribbons, and other objects that represented who we were. This mandala was in the center of our gatherings. As I began to feel stronger, our purpose expanded to include "healing" for all of us, so we met less often but for longer periods of time. Sometimes we gathered in twos and threes. The eldest of our circle died of cancer in 2002, and we all gathered at her memorial service in a weather-beaten, stained-glass-windowed church in Oakland.

On this May morning, we wanted to see who we were now and who we might yet become. As each woman spoke, I sank more deeply and quietly into the clarity of who we were together. This was how our gatherings always affected me.

Brenda spoke of having finally learned to be this "impossible thing" that she is, without masks or personas. Karen described living in the natural current of giving and receiving. Marion acknowledged being able to show the way to people through how she is in the world rather than through what she does. And Cathy, now "humbled and hewn" from years of inner work with herself and her family, said that grace was flowing in her life.

When it came my turn to speak, I heard the surprising news of my soul. "You came to me in my darkest hour. You helped me heal myself and, more important, know that I could. I felt and feel loved for who I am, right now. You helped me break my family's pattern of self-diminishment. Through your questioning and listening, you have helped me cherish who I am."

In our chapel of friendship, each gathering was a spot of grace. We created a web of tender and spacious respect that now extends across more than two decades, multiple miles, and many deaths, births, marriages, and illnesses. We ended our circle by taking apart the medicine wheel, to open space for the new and for what we might yet become.

When I started junior high in a new town, I had always been overweight, uncoordinated, and quiet. While this new beginning enabled me to start over, I still carried the same inadequate self-image and insecurities despite having lost much of the weight. I did not feel particularly likable, much less lovable. I thought I was the type of person who might be fun to be with in a moment but whose absence would go unnoticed.

Then I met a guy named John, who was tall, athletic, good looking, and filled with a generous spirit that matched his bouncy walk. One day he came up to me with great concern, asking how I was and where I had been the previous day. I was shocked! I didn't think anyone would notice or care whether I showed up or not. His act of noticing my absence and expressing how important I was to him made me feel like a real person — a whole person, not a transparent object. Our friendship solidified into a very special one, and he remains a beloved brother of my heart.

The second moment happened when my husband and I were young newlyweds, filled with excitement about our future. We were settled into a long flight from Australia to our honeymoon destination in Hawaii. The movie on the flight was about a young

People deal too much with the negative, with what is wrong.... Why not try and see positive things, to just touch those things and make them bloom?

THICH NHAT HANH

couple like ourselves who married and grew up but whose relationship over time became strained and broken. It ended with their leaving one another. As the credits rolled, I turned to my husband, who had tears running down his cheek, the first tears I had ever seen him shed. He looked at me and said, "I can't imagine ever losing you." I was overwhelmed by the depth of his love for me and recognized that I must be worthy somehow of being so cherished.

Both of these men, in these two very different moments, have caused me to search for the unique grace in my heart and come to trust the value of its simple presence.

FULL CIRCLE

BEATRICE RICH • *New York, New York*

When I was in high school, our art teacher took us to a gallery in Miami. I saw a painting that really impressed me by an artist named Eugene Massin. Not long after, as I was registering for college, the school's art instructors all sat at a table, handling the paperwork for class enrollment. The line I chose was the longest. The professor at the head of it had, for some indescribable reason, caught my attention. When I finally reached the front, I said that I wanted to study with Eugene Massin, who was a well-known Florida artist on the faculty. The instructor looked up. He was tall and broad with thick, wavy black hair and an imposing mustache. In a deep, melodic voice he told me that he was Gene Massin.

He was a dynamic, charismatic man and a great teacher. He taught me to look at things as if I had a brand-new pair of eyes — shapes, shadows, space, proportion — and to go deep inside myself to bring forward what was there. He was also rigorous. I had a facile drawing style that I had always relied on, but he wouldn't let me get away with just being charming. He chided me when I was lazy and guided me — dare I say artfully — through the rest of my years as a student.

Over the years, I kept in touch with Gene and his family. A children's book I created, *Vanessa and the Angel*, was dedicated to him. Gene loved it, and that thrilled me. The teacher was satisfied with the work of the pupil. We had come full circle.

82

The last time I saw him, he was in a wheelchair sitting at his table, still painting. He died shortly after that. His death was the hardest I have ever had to face, after the loss of my mother. I felt like an orphan all over again. But his imprint remains with me. There are two things for which I shall always be grateful: that I had the good fortune to know Gene, and that I had the intuition to stand in the longest line.

seed

MOTHER'S MANTRA

JO PEASE • *Houston, Texas*

My mother grew up during the Depression on a farm in rural Louisiana. Her father died when she was nine, and she was one of six children her mother raised alone. Life was truly difficult. She had to go to work right out of high school to support herself. She worked hard for little money. When I was growing up, therefore, my mom had little sympathy for whining. She used to say over and over and over, "Be the best that you can be. Work hard, study hard, quit your whining."

As a grown woman, I carried that mantra everywhere with me. It went round and round in my head. I could never let up because being the best that I could be was a constant challenge. I was never good enough in my own eyes because I always felt as if I could do more and be better. Work hard, study hard, and do not whine.

Shortly before my mother's death, she and I had a heart-to-heart talk. I was concerned that I had disappointed her because I had never had children. In an amazing moment, she took my hand and said, "You are the best, and I love you very much." Finally, the mantra stopped. I could rest. I knew that to her I was special. My heart began to sing, and it hasn't stopped since.

A LIGHT TO FOLLOW

MRS. ROSSI DAVIS • *Snellville, Georgia*

One person who has remained in my mind my whole life is a teacher I had as a child in Bulgaria. I do not recall many of my teachers, but she is the exception. Her name was Sylvia Grudkova. She touched me through the warmth of her heart. In the Communist country I grew up in, people had the tendency to see children as extensions of their parents. If parents had views that differed from those of the Communist government, or if they were seen as nonconformists, which mine were, things could be really difficult for the child.

As a result, some teachers treated certain children in school differently, or should I say indifferently. A child always knows when she is being ignored or made invisible. This is why Mrs. Grudkova, who was my literature teacher in the mideighties, was so important. She made me feel special because of what I had inside me rather than because of external things I had no control over.

Something in me knew she was a different type of person from the moment she came to teach our class. She was patient, warm, and present, and she didn't project an "I am the authority and you're the pupil" attitude, which most teachers did. She was mindful of how she interacted with others, nonjudgmental, and approachable as a human being. She touched the place in me that was a bare and innocent soul and encouraged me to write from that place.

I was fortunate to have her as my teacher for a few years, and then one day I was told she had to leave because her husband had

seed

gotten a job in another town. Years later, in 1992, I was in Bulgaria's capital, Sofia, prior to coming to the United States. My grandmother and I were crossing a busy street. I looked up, and there was Mrs. Grudkova crossing the street! She did not see me; nor did I flag her down. We were rushing, caught in the moment, but my soul recognized her. I remember that image, since it was one of the last things I saw before leaving Bulgaria.

To deny that we are gifted is, perhaps, to indulge in false humility, which allows us to shirk our responsibility to the gift. . . . Gifts must be developed and passed on.

DEENA METZGER

Later, when I had the opportunity to teach in college, I remembered this most influential teacher and the effect she had on my life. The place she recognized in me has become the light I follow. I do my best to find it in every student I work with.

PLAYING FOR HER

CATHERINE DESANTIS • *Arcata, California*

I am sitting in my mother's lap. It is wide and soft and warm. When she kisses my cheek and wraps her arms around me, I am enclosed in a soft universe.

I was one of five children to share her lap, and she had only so much energy to give, but she carved out quiet time with each of us, and it was so sweet. During one of those moments, she had settled in to do a huge pile of ironing — my father wore white, starched shirts — but before she started she invited me to put my little hands on a coffee table so she could paint my fingernails. She told me that my fingers were long and slender, just perfect for playing music if that's what I wanted to do. She knew I adored listening to music and singing, but I had never thought I could actually grow up to be a musician.

A few years later she bought me my first flute and drove me back and forth to lessons. I remember the look on her face when she listened to me rehearse. The corners of her mouth turned up, and her eyes glowed with awe.

I was with my mother when she died. She stayed present through the three days of hard work that it took for her to cross over. I sang to her, and I played my flute for her. Now, whenever I play, I honor her love for me, and her recognizing my gift. Her name was Eugenie Josephine LaMean.

seed

"MEAN AND ORNERY" DOESN'T LAST FOREVER

ANDY BRYNER • *Geyserville, California*

Recently, when people ask my eighty-eight-year-old father how he is, he replies, "Mean and ornery." He certainly does have those traits. He says it is his stubborn German blood. So it was surprising when we had a conversation that seemed out of character for him.

Long before, when I was five, he called me into the room he called his den. This is where he administered his duties as a rural justice of the peace. He made me stand in front of him and look him very seriously in the eye. Then he said, "My dad and I could never talk. So I want you to know that you can come to me anytime you want, and we can talk."

In the years after, it turned out that almost every time we talked it had to do with a mistake I had made or how I had done things the wrong way. Even though his critiques were all "for my own good," they were very uncomfortable. "For my own good" came to mean "for my own pain." As much as I admired some aspects of my dad and wanted to please him, I started to avoid conversation and real contact with him. That went on for many years — decades, actually.

So you can imagine how surprised I was when he, now eighty-eight, said to me, "If you ever have a problem or need advice, talk to me about it." I had heard that part before, but

> *When beauty touches our lives, the moment becomes luminous. These grace-moments are gifts that surprise us.*
>
> JOHN O'DONOHUE

spot of grace

never what he said next. "You don't have to take my advice. Do whatever you believe is best, but it's always good to ask for the thinking of others."

I slept on those words, and the next day I took a gamble. I asked his advice about a career change I was thinking about making. His response blew me away: "Figure out what you love and what you are good at. Then do more of that."

In that moment, my "mean and ornery" dad became the dad that I once adored, the dad for whose praise I had searched all those years. Instead of demanding I work harder to be better, he had finally, in that moment, blessed my spot of grace and encouraged me to set it free.

seed

flower

Who Stands Beside You?

A self is made, not given. It is a creative and active process
of attending a life that must be heard, shaped, seen,
said aloud into the world, finally enacted and woven into the lives of others.

BARBARA MYERHOFF, *Remembered Lives*

My grandmother was a tiny woman, shrunken as if some of the juice had been sucked out of her. But her hands, her timeless, precious hands, were an entire landscape, the veins risen to the surface, a network of rivers that flowed from her heart. Her long white fingers were rooted in the wisdom of escorting babies into the world and dying people out of it. When she was telling stories to explain things to me, these root-fingers seemed to point to what was buried beneath the surface of ordinary things. One Sunday she drew a large spiral slowly in the air and called it the Wisdom Trail.

"Each of us travels this path, round and round the spot of grace at our core. As we do, we come to the same intersections, the same challenges, over and over," she said softly.

Transfixed, I saw what she spoke of in the air in front of us. The taxi horns, the pigeon wings flapping outside the window, the pizza smells from Esposito's restaurant downstairs all disappeared as Grandma's words carried me into the middle of this spiral.

"People walk this trail shifting from one foot to the other — first a step of risk to learn something new; then a step of mastery so they can live what they've learned. If they use only their foot of risk, they spend their lives hopping nervously from thing to thing. But if they use only their foot of mastery, they get stuck and stagnant."

Kneeling on the floor next to her in the kitchen while she made bread for the Sabbath, I watched my grandmother's floury hands leave prints on the red oilcloth–covered table as they walked across, illustrating the story.

"Sometimes people might think they are going in circles, never making progress, even moving backward, but that's not true. It's just that each pass around, you gather more wisdom, so your trail is wider, and you travel it with more grace from risk to mastery to risk again."

She leaned toward me and whispered, "What's important," — Grandma tapped the end of my nose with one dusty finger and then continued — "is that, whichever foot you use to walk this path, remember that there's no way to escape from yourself or what you came here to do."

> *Freedom is not given to us by anyone; we have to cultivate it ourselves. It is a daily practice. . . . When you eat, eat as a free person. When you walk, walk as a free person. When you breathe, breathe as a free person. This is possible anywhere. No one can prevent you from enjoying the bite of food you take. No one can prevent you from being aware of each step you take or each breath in and each breath out. Everyone walks on this earth, but there are those who walk like slaves, with no freedom at all. If we get caught up in our worries and fear of the future, our regrets about the past, we are not free people.*
>
> THICH NHAT HANH

BEAUTIFULLY SPOKEN SILENCE

CHRIS AMOROSO, MD • *Green Valley, Arizona*

My forty-one-year-old daughter, Yarra, for ten years had been challenged with progressive, disabling multiple sclerosis. For the past three years she had been unable to eat, move her body, or speak. I read newspapers, poems, and books to her, played music, told stories, or made funny faces — anything I could think of to connect with her, to evoke a knowing look in her eyes, a responsive laugh or sound of some sort. I psyched myself up for the visits, hoping to share a few moments of joy. Most days there was no response.

One day, bone tired and resting quietly in the chair by her bedside, I realized my breathing was synchronized with the rhythm of her breathing. I then began to notice that silence was being spoken beautifully between and around us. In her motionless, speechless soulfulness, Spirit filled the room. As I gazed around, I realized the room was full of her brightly colored art, which had been produced with the one arm that could move partially during the early years of the MS. Back then, Yarra had said over and over, "Okay, life, give me what you've got. I will take it and make it mine. I will transform it into my beautiful world. Thank you, thank you, thank you!"

I looked at her still body. A serenity and radiance shone forth from her. There was an energy field in her room that invited me to take a healing break. Creativity was alive there, when I paused to look and listen to it and let it connect to my spirit. Even when I left the room, this peaceful satisfaction stayed with me.

flower

I marvel at how she responded to the challenges life brought her. Indeed, she had MS, and it didn't have her. I have come to realize that having a severely afflicted daughter is one of my own life challenges. I can't be so busy dealing with the challenges life brings me that I forget to make my own world beautiful. Creativity must be alive in me, and I must pause to look for it, listen to it, and let it connect to my spirit. Yarra taught me that it is the pauses between the notes that help make the miraculous music of life come alive.

It is one of the extraordinary gifts of life that we can choose our traveling companions, those we love and whose company we keep. Since childhood, I have lived and moved with more joy and freedom when I am riding large creatures endowed with hooves and flowing tails. I choose to keep the company of horses.

This is a story about the death of one such horse: Hubba Bubba, my snow-white friend who stayed with me for seventeen years. In those years we jumped, rode miles upon miles of trails, and tried our hand at such far-ranging disciplines as barrel racing and the high art of dressage. In truth, we excelled at none of those sports. What Hubba Bubba excelled at was something beyond skill or expertise. His bravery could not be developed. He was born with it.

On a warm November afternoon in his twenty-second year, Hubba Bubba could barely take a step. A massive infection had set in, and the vet, seeing that no more could be done, asked if I wanted to end his suffering with a humane injection. It might have been the most appropriate path, but Hubba Bubba's brown eyes were still aware and curious, as if asking, "What next?"

I asked the vet to come back in the morning, saying I wanted to give my companion the night. After he left, Hubba Bubba continued looking past the open stall door, out to the grassy field and the lake beyond. Then he stepped forward past the stall door. I watched, amazed, as Bubba moved forward, stiff for sure, but each hoof placed

flower

97

carefully, step by step, as if knowing exactly where he wanted go. In the last of daylight, he stopped at the very edge of the pasture, looking to the great flock of Canada geese and traveling birds.

Only then did I realize I had a big bag of carrots in my hand. I offered him one, then two, his usual reward. I'll never forget how he looked at me as I went to put the bag down and stop feeding him. A thought popped into my mind: "If he eats them all, what's it gonna do? Kill him?"

I picked up the bag and fed him every carrot. He chewed slowly, as if enjoying each bite. By the time he was finished, the harvest moon was well over the field.

When I came back in the morning, he was gone at the edge of the pasture, a last lying down. Hubba Bubba's eye was closed, an empty carrot bag discarded by his side. The morning brought a cool, fresh breeze, and rather than being sad, I felt warmed by a feeling of composure and tenderness. I thought, "This is right. This is how it is supposed to be."

Without words, this horse had taught me, not in one moment but in a lifetime of moments, that I could be brave enough, like him, to embrace the process of living and dying.

> *Hold onto what is good*
> *even if it is a handful of earth.*
> *Hold onto what you believe*
> *even if it is a tree that stands by itself.*
> *Hold onto what you must do*
> *even if it is a long way from here.*
> *Hold onto life*
> *even when it is easier letting go.*
> *Hold onto my hand*
> *even when I have gone away from you.*
>
> PUEBLO BLESSING

THE LIGHT MY MOTHER SAW

KITTY PLATT • *Omaha, Nebraska*

I sat in a room with my mother and my two sisters. My younger sister, Leah, was a smiling, glowing three-year-old cocoa mix of my mother and . . . some man. The doctors said that she would never talk — too much deformation in her jaw and brain damage from everything my mother had consumed and endured while she was pregnant. My older sister, Debbie, was ten, defiant and full of anger. She had lived through ten surgeries and had a colostomy bag that was never really kept clean, but that was the least of the damage she'd suffered. And I was the girl in the middle. I was healthy. Maybe that was luck, or maybe it was the product of the guilt my mother had suffered over my sister, which had kept her clean while she was pregnant with me. Maybe I was something that came from a happier time in her life. That's the best story I can tell myself. My mother told us that Social Services and the police had asked her to sign a paper that said that she would never see us again. She asked us what we wanted her to do. There was so much pain in her eyes, but her voice was clear, unshaken.

"No! F--- them!" Debbie screamed, throwing her chair to the side of the room.

My mother kept her eyes on me. I think she knew I had become wiser than my six years.

"Let us go," I whispered.

She signed the papers. That was the last time I ever saw her.

flower

I didn't know what was ahead of me, but I knew there had to be something better than what I'd seen so far. I loved my mother more than anything in this world. I wasn't angry with her. We understood each other. I knew I needed to let her go as much as she needed to let me go. To this day, I don't have bad memories of her, only love.

I was finally adopted when I was thirteen. When I was seventeen, my adopted parents told me that my mother had gotten drunk, fallen down some stairs, and just died after being in a coma. I was the only living relative that could be found who had the capacity to release her remains to her boyfriend. Every bone of my body shook with impotent rage. I never got the chance to tell her why I had made the choice that I did that day. I never got the chance to tell her that I loved her, that I wasn't angry at her, and that I had never felt any disappointment toward her. I had planned on finding her when I was older. I had planned on showing her what I'd been able to become because of who she had made me and because she knew to let me go. What if she didn't understand all this? What if I could have been there when she was in a coma? What if it were true that people can hear you when they're in a coma and maybe sometimes it can make them come out of it?

A couple weeks later, I wrote my entrance essay for Columbia University about my early history and my mother's death. I was determined that my mother would watch me shine from wherever she was. The university wanted to interview me, but I didn't have enough money to go. Even so, I imagined that Columbia had seen in me what my mother saw. It helped me keep on keeping on. I wanted to be a writer, but I ended up becoming something more "sensible." For over twelve years I went to community colleges and the state university at night while working by day.

> *The most invisible creators I know of are those artists whose medium is life itself. The ones who express the inexpressible — without brush, hammer, clay or guitar. They neither paint nor sculpt — their medium is their being. Whatever their presence touches has increased life. They see and don't have to draw. They are the artists of being alive.*
>
> J. STONE

I realized this morning that I have worked every day at trying to get others to see in me the light that my mother saw. I have wanted that so badly. I have refused to become what I saw as failure. I refused to let foster homes that didn't want me make me stumble. I moved on. I refused to let companies that didn't see what I had to offer hold me back. I moved on. I refused to let friends who didn't want to have reciprocal relationships get in my way. I moved on. I refused to stay with a husband who couldn't value me and my daughter over his drugs. I moved on, hoping that someday someone would see this light in me. And maybe I didn't really live, but I survived, wanting everyone to see in me what I needed to see in myself.

I'm now a thirty-eight-year-old professional, a CPA, a former CFO, a former... many things. I've always worked hard and given everything I had and yet felt empty. I'm always searching for that something that will make me complete. I heard a speech the other day by a woman at a leadership conference. She said, "I know you have a spot of grace. Never before and never again will there be one such as you. No one else carries the one-of-a-kind gift, the talents, skills, experiences, and passions that you possess."

While I was lying in bed this morning thinking about all of this, my four-year-old son came and lay down next to me. What will he see in me? What will all my children see? The stress and the bickering with my husband? Mommy working all the time? Or will they see in me that spot of grace that I saw in my mother and she saw in me? What am I doing to grow it in me and in them?

The sun is coming up. It's beautiful. Today is a different day. It's the first day, not of survival, but of life.

WORTH FIGHTING FOR

MARY E. GUIBERSON • *Seattle, Washington*

On September 24, as I lay wanting to die in the house on Delridge, most of what I knew or believed about the world was dying with my addiction. At that moment I could never have envisioned the life I have today with a community that means so much to me. The only things holding me here were my heart, my will to live, and the prayers from my angels.

I was in the middle of a spiritual birth. I had to surrender my life to the care of others that day and the three days that followed. On the fourth day, my friend Carl woke me up and told me that I had a temperature of 106, and he thought I should go to the hospital immediately. I agreed, figuring I would get up and go by myself. That was how I had lived my life for the past five years, on the streets as an addict: by myself.

Much to my surprise, Carl called the ambulance, sat on the sidewalk with me waiting for them to come, got into the vehicle, and came with me to the hospital. He did not leave my side that Monday night until I was tucked into my room on the fourth floor of Harborview Medical Center. When Carl finally did go, he handed me a small gold heart as he walked out the door. He never returned, but the gift he gave me stays with me to this day. He made me feel that my life was worth fighting for, that I was someone who matters.

flower

"They'll win. Trust me," she said.

"They're down 3–0," I replied. "To the Yankees. No one's ever come back from that — not in baseball, not in any professional sport. Certainly not to the Yankees. It's not gonna happen. Game over."

How could I explain this to my wife? Never a sports fan, she nonetheless put up with my stormy emotions over the years, giving me space after a loss and knowing I'd bounce back. But there would be no recovery this time; my faith had been pushed too far, and the Red Sox were never going to win for me.

I rolled back over in bed, knowing there would be not a wink of sleep, that visions of every other miserable end to a Red Sox season would dance in my head 'til morning. I had cried myself to sleep as a nine-year-old when they lost the '75 World Series to the Reds. I had bruised my hand punching a wall when Bucky F---ing Dent ended their dream season in '78. I had drunk half a bottle of gin and sobbed for hours with my friend Hench when they lost to the Mets in the '86 series. And I had puked my guts out when they somehow lost the seventh game of the ALCS against those same Yankees the year before after Grady Little left Pedro in an inning too long. My friends think I take this team too seriously, but everybody needs something to believe in.

"I can feel it — they're really going to do it," Angie said. "Just because no one's ever done it before it'll be that much more special."

Over the next several days I didn't dare to hope, but slowly it was happening. Game 4: Big Papi won it in the twelfth. Game 5: Papi again in the fourteenth. Game 6: Schilling's heroic effort on a bloody, surgically repaired ankle. Game 7: a blur as they pounded the Yankees in their own house, 7–3. The World Series itself was an afterthought. The Red Sox Nation was in pandemonium. Watching the parade in Boston, hearing tales of lifelong Sox fans in their nineties who finally got to see them win after a lifetime of bitterness, washed away decades of disappointment in streams of joyous tears.

It doesn't matter that they'd break my heart again the next year in the '05 playoffs. It's not a big deal that Pedro, Derek Lowe, and Johnny Damon would all leave for other teams. I've seen the impossible once in my lifetime. While I'm no less manic about the Sox than ever, the 2004 miracle season helped me: 1) learn to be as loyal to whatever I love as my wife is to me; 2) pay attention to her intuition even when it makes no rational sense — and consider that I may have some intuition too; and 3) believe that someday, somehow, I'll have a chance to do something exceptional, something inspiring, even in the face of such an overwhelming force as the Curse of the Bambino!

Cinnamon was our spirited Belgian Malinois–boxer, a loyal, jovial companion for more than a dozen years. My husband and I adopted her from a rescue agency, which informed us that she and her litter of five pups had been abandoned in the woods of the Eastern Shore.

In her later years she developed a rare condition known as canine myasthenia gravis. The illness left her unable to swallow. Conventional veterinary medications nearly killed her in the early stages of the disease. I soon sought the help of a vet who practiced alternative treatment methods. Dr. Grace treated Cinnamon with acupuncture, homeopathic medicines, and vitamin and mineral supplements. I fed Cinnamon several small, bland meals of turkey and rice each day, adding just the right concoction of homeopathic tablets and liquids and mashing them all together to a semiliquid consistency that she could slurp. I massaged her for fifteen minutes after each meal, vigilantly making sure that she sat upright and didn't lie down too soon after eating, which would have led to aspiration pneumonia and death.

For nearly two years I practiced this mealtime routine with her, until the illness finally won. Two weeks after Cinnamon's death, I received a note in the mail from Dr. Grace. She wrote about the "miracle patient" that Cinnamon was, living for almost two years with a disease that should have taken her much sooner. She noted that because of my determination and commitment to treatment, Cinnamon's life was extended so that we were able to enjoy many more happy days together. Dr. Grace pointed out that most people who have an animal with myasthenia gravis won't put that much time and effort into the animal's life; they opt for immediate euthanization. She commended me for my dedication, care, and love. Her brief note made the hole in my heart a little smaller that day. I realized that although I hadn't been able to save Cinnamon from the disease, I had respected her life and made it as comfortable as possible until the very end. Caring so deeply in this way revealed a place in me I hadn't known existed until then.

> *Seeing what is true, the heart becomes free.*
>
> SUZUKI ROSHI

flower

GAY JOHN

CHARLIE JORDAN • *Birmingham, England*

At age thirteen I was already six feet tall, wore glasses, and ate my packed lunch in the school restrooms. This was to avoid the bullies who made the lunch hall a terrifying place for those of us girls who didn't conform to the petite blue-eyed blonde stereotype. My mom was often ill, and I looked after her, which made me feel more responsible and isolated. I felt like I didn't fit in anywhere.

I experimented with making my own clothes, as I was too tall for the ready-made sizes. I created unusual shapes and colors and started to look around for inspiration. There was a huge store called Hyperactive, which was jammed with the most exotic creations I'd ever seen. It was impossibly glamorous to my eyes. I walked through it in awe of the celebratory colors, gravity-defying hats, and eclectic people. The sense of freedom was intoxicating, as was the energy of so many young, talented people trying new ideas.

On the top floor, in the café, was a DJ who kept up a buzzing atmosphere like a ceremonial shaman. Tall, Hollywood handsome, and wearing makeup, he called himself Gay John. And he spoke to me. Yes, me! He complimented me on my homemade outfit and made me feel welcome.

I was transformed by his kindness and hoped a touch of his glamour would rub off on me. He introduced me to some of the other characters there, and these cool, artistic men and women just chatted to me as if I belonged. Perhaps in my awkward teenage self they recognized

spot of grace

something of their own experience of looking a bit different. Black, white, or dual heritage; gay or straight; tattooed, pierced, bald, or dreadlocked — we were all different. But uniqueness was celebrated and interesting.

I doubt John ever realized how those few minutes of his time helped me to feel accepted.

We were a tribe of wonderful misfits. I worked a few Saturdays there and in the bar next door, and I even modeled for some of the designers in local fashion shows. Being six feet tall was a bonus now, and gradually my confidence increased.

I outgrew the bitchy girls. They had no power to hurt me anymore, and the bullying eased off. I've never forgotten what it felt like to be the odd one out and will always go out of my way to include anyone who seems to feel like one. My career as a radio presenter has enabled me to help many "odd ones" tell their story. I feel so lucky that my work allows freedom of expression. I feel very blessed and want you to know that angels can sometimes wear eyeliner. Thank you, Gay John.

I sat in a circle of a hundred women, who had gathered for a week to be in silence and meaningful conversation with author and philosopher Joanna Macy. I was there to grieve my sister's imminent passing. We all were there to repurpose and reengage our lives.

This Thursday morning we formed what Joanna called a Truth Mandala. She walked from one quadrant to another, dropping in each an object that represented one of four emotions: anger, fear, despair, and sorrow. She said each of these emotions had a hidden partner. The other side of anger is passion. The other side of fear is courage. The other side of grief is rebirth, and the other side of sorrow is love. In the center of the circle was hope. Joanna explained the process we would follow: each of us who felt so moved would come one at a time and stand in the quadrant that represented the emotion we needed to speak from, to share the truth of our own experience or that of another who was not in the room. "The rest of you," she said turning slowly and looking at each woman in the circle, "are here with and for each other. You will participate through your listening to and bearing witnesses for the woman in the center."

I had no intention of speaking. I had been public far too much. I had come to this workshop to crawl into the concave surface of my heart and prepare for my sister's death. I sat listening for over two hours, absorbing the stories, holding each woman in the cradle of my attention. The last woman to speak was dressed like a living flame, her skin as dark as wood. A fury burned through her as she screamed that none of us could understand what it felt like to be a black woman in America. Pointing at each one of us, she shouted, "Don't tell me you are my sister! You are not my sister!"

> *Our individuality is all, all, that we have. There are those who barter it for security, those who repress it for what they believe is the betterment of the whole society, but blessed in the twinkle of the morning star is the one who nurtures and rides it, in grace and love and wit, from peculiar station to peculiar station along life's bittersweet route.*
>
> TOM ROBBINS

When she sat down on the other side of the circle, a river broke inside my body, the way the frozen rivers in Vermont crack when spring comes. Its current dragged me shaking into the circle. A flood of words came rushing through me, carrying the debris of my fifteen-year-old self, violated in every opening of her body. I was not speaking the words. They were raging through me.

"Passion is the other side of anger? Courage, the other side of fear? Rebirth, the other side of grief? Love, the other side of sorrow?" Each question crashed against the shore of the women sitting around me. "Well, then, tell me, all of you, tell me, what is the other side of rape?"

The voice that was birthing itself through my throat was not only my voice. It flowed from Auschwitz and the Sudan, from Bosnia and Harlem, from Baghdad and Calcutta. It rose and roared from the hundred and sixty million "untouchables" in India who now call themselves the Dalits, "those broken to pieces." They do not own land, attend school, or drink from the same wells as those "higher" than them. They are brutalized and raped at will.

The current carried me from quadrant to quadrant, and then, at last, into the center of the circle. I turned to face the woman who had spoken before me. I extended my arm toward her, pointed my index finger directly at her, felt my voice resonating one word after another through every fiber of my body: "And ... you ... are ... my ... sister!" Her arms opened, and our separate hearts, each a refugee, found their twin. All those women I had spoken for were cradled in our embrace.

Sometimes all I can offer to life is my tears. That afternoon, as I wrote in my journal and walked in silence on a parched Northern California hillside, my tears became a stream of ink:

> What is the soul leakage that causes us to divide and degrade each other so? I don't know the big answer. I don't understand the cultural, historical, and religious implications of the question. I only know that if I listen deeply enough, my soul replies, "But when are *you* the perpetrator, my dearest one? To find the other side of rape, you must let these questions be your crucible: What are the broken pieces in your life that you have made untouchable? What do you, with the power of your will and the brilliance of your 'higher' mind, divide off from your life and degrade? What school do you not allow your heart to attend? What is its native land that you have disowned? And hardest of all to consider, my darling, what is there in your heart that you have raped and brutalized and that cries out now to be healed?"

There is a bridge woven out of strands invisible to the ordinary eye between my own life and every person anywhere who has been raped. I found the other side of that bridge while walking on the hillside, when my soul challenged me to recognize that the bridge was also a connection of deep understanding to every perpetrator of rape.

Walking that California hillside bleached white in the summer sun, I knew that I would never forget that I carry within me the best and the worst of what it is possible for a human to do. Gratitude rose in the center of my chest for all the people, opportunities, and choices that have been my handholds in the darkness.

I was sitting, defeated, on Silver Rock beach in southern Barbados. My husband, Dave, and I had come to windsurf and celebrate his fortieth birthday. I had just spent my first session getting pummeled, trying to carry my gear through the huge shore break. The five meters of sail had gotten caught in the current and pulled me under. There was no way I could lift the sail enough to take off. I clung to the mast, watching the colorful banners of the equipment-rental shop getting smaller and smaller on the horizon. I was quickly being carried farther down the shoreline. I used every muscle fiber I had to lift the sail, but I was hopeless against the waves and the weight of my rig. The shop sent out one of its instructors to help me. Humiliated, I made it back to where I could stand and did the walk of shame back to the windsurf hut.

I had been out there trying to survive for only a half hour, but it felt like half of my life. Sitting on the white sand, my eyes stinging, my nose dripping all the saltwater I had inhaled, I felt useless and heartless.

I began to watch a young local boy jump in the waves. His dirty white boxers got pulled down on each jump, but he didn't care. He was ecstatic with each wave. Occasionally he tried to swim, his arms and legs slapping and flapping out of control. After each attempt, half drowning, he pulled his head up and grinned, looking at a woman who sat on a broken chair at an empty hotel on the beach.

spot of grace

He was irresistible. Though I am generally nervous talking to kids I don't know well, I decided to go join him. I jumped with him a couple of times and soon became his wave playmate. Between sets, he told me the whole history of the island, including amazing facts from his lineage of fisherman. His Barbadian accent made me smile. I learned his name was Tevin, and he was on school break. Other kids in the neighborhood called him "Fat One." He didn't want to get involved with bad kids because he promised his mom he would do well in school. I asked if the woman in the chair was his mother. He said yes and explained that she was the security guard for the abandoned hotel, and she brought him to the beach so she could watch him while she worked. She didn't know how to swim and was afraid of the water, so he could play only when others were on the beach. I wondered what it must be like for her to live on this beautiful island with its long blue-green beaches, knowing that if something happened, she could not help him.

> *Everyone has inside of him a piece of good news. The good news is that you don't know how great you can be! How much you can love! What you can accomplish! And what your potential is!*
>
> ANNE FRANK

Over the next hour I taught Tevin to swim. I showed him how to tread water, how to cup his hands, how to use his arms and legs. I told him he was lucky to be big because it helped him float better. His grin grew even wider as he proudly displayed his twelve-year-old body.

He was an anxious, determined student, standing up after three strokes and asking, "Was dat good, mon?" Eventually, we both grew

flower

happily tired. He wanted to rest; "relaxin'" was good for the heart and a pastime as necessary to Barbadians as eating. I returned to the spot on the beach next to my limp rig, and Tevin ran in his soggy boxers back to his mother, who energetically waved at me while patting her son on the back.

I caught a glimpse of Dave's sail gliding across the ocean. The windsurf rig that nearly drowned me was a wing of grace for him. The waves that pummeled and suffocated me were launch pads for his breathtaking jumps and head-over-heels loops.

I grabbed my rig, rested it on my hip, and walked back into the shore break. I looked back at Tevin, who gave me a wide and enthusiastic grin. I looked at the waves and decided I would try this again, with "Tevin attitude," grinning no matter what.

During my week in Barbados, I spent more time jumping and swimming with Tevin. Each day he ran up to me, shouting, "Ms. Angie, I been practicing." He would proudly show me his new confident stroke. He pointed to Dave and excitedly tried to guess when he was going to jump. He declared that now that he knew how to swim, he was going to learn to sail like us.

I taught him to swim, but by shining the light of that joyful heart on my broken spirit, Tevin taught me to play — and that gave me all the buoyancy I needed to get out and sail again.

DANGLING

COURTNEY A. WALSH • *Woonsocket, Rhode Island*

My feet are dangling in the water of my best friend's pool. An oily slick of dead bugs and leaves is swirling on the surface, and I'm mesmerized by the play of light and shadow and by the circular movement of my feet in the water.

It's my twenty-first summer, and my best friend's father has recently hanged himself, causing us all to stop in shock and wonder at his lonely death in a crappy, dark basement, surrounded by empty beer cans and a lifetime of disappointment — a stark contrast to these gorgeous, blue-sky summer days.

At the funeral, my friend seemed so much older than her nineteen years. Sorrow had literally aged her overnight so that she seemed more like a bent-over, grieving Italian war widow than the bubbly cheerleader I'd known for years. Her brother, a few years older, bore her up as they received the waves of relatives they had met only once or, in some cases, never. Their mother had died of cancer when they were in elementary school. They were now young adult orphans, having to face the world and survive the ultimate shame, a family member's suicide. The word was never spoken, except in hushed whispers at the edges of the cloyingly scented, flower-filled room.

Hoping to bring myself back to my body and its solid aliveness, I swish these thoughts around in my head as my feet do their egg-beater dance in the water, banging occasionally against the concrete edge. A dragonfly lies on the water's surface, struggling with a broken

flower

117

wing, drowning as it struggles. I scoop it up with both hands, pouring it onto the concrete. There is nothing else I can do except watch as it dies. Like my friend's dad, it was lost the moment it hit the water.

> *I want to do with you what spring does with the cherry trees.*
>
> PABLO NERUDA

By cutting his life short by his own hand, my friend's father inadvertently taught me that every moment matters. He taught me that there is no such thing as too many I-love-yous. He taught me that even a final act of selfishness or desperation can contain a gift. Since that day, my feet are not dangling. My prayer is to live better, love stronger, and plant both feet firmly on the earth while reaching both wings toward the sky.

HALF AND HALF EQUALS TWO WHOLES

J. R. • *Oregon*

I donated half of my liver to my daughter. The decision to do it was easy. I was a match, my daughter was dying, and I could save her life. I didn't think much about the risks. I didn't really want to know about how it would affect me. I avoided articles about long recoveries or complications. After all, my daughter had been sick for most of her thirteen years of life, and her needs have always come first. I never thought about my own.

We secured the hospital and transplant team, set the date, and counted the days until she would have relief for her emaciated, jaundiced body. I went into surgery still joking and smiling, relieved that the wait was nearly over. The morning after our ten-hour transplant, all I wanted to know was how my daughter was doing. Was she better? Alert? Breathing okay? In pain? I was getting an update on her condition, looking at a few digital pictures, when a shot of pain took hold of me and wouldn't let go. I literally could not breathe. Breaking out in a sweat, I cried for relief and called for the nurse.

Thirty minutes and several medications later I could breathe again, but I also had a new perspective on our situation. I had been selfless for thirteen years in order to take care of my daughter. No one else could have given her what I did. With each breath, I began to realize that I too had intrinsic value. I had to put myself first for a while and take time to heal. I was the patient now, and what was important was preventing blood clots and infections and caring for my

flower

119

lungs and digestive tract. I had to mother myself. Before long I was able to take my first steps. Then the time came for my first ride in a wheelchair to look into my daughter's eyes and hear her whisper, "Oh, Mommy, I love you."

Two weeks later we were both discharged from the hospital and I was holding her in my arms. Now, six months later, when I see her run and laugh, my heart fills with joy. She's made it, I've made it, and we're moving on. Not only does she have a new life that matters; so do I.

REDEMPTION

DANA BOALES • *Tacoma, Washington*

When I was twelve years old my mother married James. He was a machinist, a Vietnam veteran, and a survivor of many years of domestic violence at the hands of his father. James was a drinker who loved to party, laugh, and joke. The marriage lasted only eight years and produced my brother, Jade, and sister, Jennifer. After the divorce my stepfather had no contact with Jennifer and Jade for more than a decade. He missed birthdays, holidays, and graduations. He did attend my sister's wedding and my brother's graduation, which occurred on the same day. He then lost contact again.

Three years ago we received news that James was dying and wanted to see his children and new granddaughter, Maya Olivia. He lived in east Texas, many hours from the south Texas town where my family now lives. I was in Seattle. As I had grown older and wiser, my adolescent anger with James had been transformed to a deep sympathy. Whenever I thought of him, my heart was filled with compassion.

When I heard his request, I knew that this was a journey that my brother and sister and I had to make together. Jade and Jennifer needed to do this as an act of forgiveness; I needed to make the journey as an act of contrition. We all needed to participate in the healing. When I asked, my siblings responded without hesitation and agreed to meet me in Houston to make the long drive to east Texas. They did not have much money, so I assured them that if they could make it to Houston, I would take care of the rest.

flower

121

We found James gaunt and eaten up by cancer. Nonetheless, my usually reserved niece, Maya, sat in his lap as if she had done so her whole life. We stayed the weekend, sharing a small hotel room in a town adjacent to his. Our weekend was filled with laughter, beer, and the knowledge that this would likely be the last time that we would all be together.

James died a month later, on Christmas Eve. He was buried on New Year's Eve. My mother joked, "Leave it to James to try to up-stage the holidays." I couldn't go to the funeral, but that didn't matter. My brother went and rang in the new year with his many cousins at James's favorite watering hole. What did matter was that through compassion and forgiveness, we had helped him end his life in cele-bration. For me, making a difference can be as simple and as difficult as opening your heart.

HARBOR ME

RACHEL EDWARDS • *Rochester, New York*

As a college student, I took a camping trip with my Italian friend, Cristina, along the Dalmatian coast of what was then Yugoslavia. Visiting a friend near Dubrovnik, we left our gear in her garage while we went into town for some dinner and sightseeing. When we returned that night, we were greeted by lights, sirens, and emergency workers shouting in a language we couldn't understand.

> *Blessed is the influence of one true, loving, human soul on another.*
>
> GEORGE ELIOT

Apparently, our friend's boyfriend had been working on his motorcycle in the garage when something had ignited a spark and his hands, covered in gasoline, began to burn. As he ran across the street to put out the flames in the ocean, he was struck by a hit-and-run driver and killed. The garage had burned to the ground, with our possessions among the unfathomable loss.

I had never experienced this kind of devastation before. The world became a hostile place. We limped, in shock, back to Italy. We were greeted by Cristina's family, who enveloped us in unconditional love. They offered us a refuge as well as the time and space to digest what had happened on what was supposed to be a lark of a camping trip. Aunts and uncles replaced many of our lost items. This was a family whose home had been occupied by German officers during World War II. Their hearts had been tested by hardships, and they poured out exactly what we most needed to heal.

flower

123

The unconditional generosity of this family I hardly knew helped me come back into the present reality, where I was safe. The family's compassion couldn't answer the endless questions we asked of why this had happened, but it served as a lasting reminder for me of the power of love to heal the tragic events we cannot control.

AND THEN WE SPOKE TOGETHER

JUANITA BROWN • *Mill Valley, California*

I am visiting with my Uncle Phil. He is dying of cancer. Phil has always said he prefers the horizontal life. He is a retired university professor. He is eccentric. He is a gregarious recluse. His small home, across the street from the Methodist Church, is cluttered. Books fill every nook and cranny — the kitchen, the bathrooms, the basement — books of Spanish literature and philosophy. Rare art books. Books of home remedies and 1960s pocket novels.

We sit on his bed together, as we did when I was a child. It is late at night. Beside the bed is a big plastic bag of candies — butterscotch, my favorites. Phil reaches into the bag. I smile and accept his offer. We begin to talk together, as we have for almost half a century, as we did when I was a small child and my mom would let me stay up late with "El Profesor." Back then we explored the forests of the unknown together. He posed questions that neither of us could answer, both of us captivated by the journey of discovery.

Tonight we are traveling together into the land of the vacuum. Looking up from the pillow, he puts his finger to his mouth, pauses, and then asks, "What is the Nothing? What can come from Nothing, and where does Nothing go?"

"Ah," I say. This is a question El Profesor and I, his favorite niece, have been exploring for many years. He has always been haunted by wondering about life's meaning, and the theme of the vacuum has been central to our conversation.

But now my Uncle Phil is dying, and we have not yet spoken of death. "Well, Uncle Phil, I finally think I know. The Nothing is the generative, nurturing vacuum — the vacuum that is not empty but that holds all, as potential, in its embrace. The Everything emerges from the Nothing. It is where life comes from and where life returns to. I used to be afraid of the vacuum, but I'm not anymore."

The room is silent. The light flickers. Phil looks at me — then closes his eyes. I wait. I touch his arm, gently. He opens his eyes. There is silence. I ask, "How did I do, Uncle Phil? I've been working on this question since I was a child. Have I been a good student?"

He smiles as if to himself. He purses his lips quizzically in deep thought. He looks up at me. There is a long silence. I wait, not touching him this time. Then, with a wry grin, he responds, "My dear, you receive an A-plus!"

We look at each other and smile. Something deep in me sighs. I touch his arm gently and go to bed. My uncle and I have spoken together.

My first teacher was Herr Dewald in the Schule Gratenstrasse in Karlsruhe, Germany. It was in the 1930s as Hitler came to power. I was Jewish and was considered therefore a second-class citizen. The other children and teachers ignored or humiliated me, but Herr Dewald protected me. He knew I loved to learn, and he poured everything he could into me, the little sponge.

One day he had to punish me for something I had done wrong. I became sick, and so did he. He held me afterward, and I knew, I just knew, that he respected me. I knew that there must be something worthy of respect inside me if Herr Dewald could feel that way.

That "something" grew even as I escaped to France. One day, Thanksgiving 1940, after my father had been sent to an internment camp, I was invited by some friends of the family, Mr. and Mrs. Kerschner, to serve at a party in their home. Mr. Kerschner began to play American spirituals on his harmonica, and my deep sadness lifted. In an atmosphere of shelter and respect, the light recognized by Herr Dewald began to shine, and I realized that music, a language without borders, could nurture it and support my being.

flower

FINDING HIM IN ME

EVA-MARIA SYDNEY • *Seehausen am Staffelsee, Germany*

I will call him Leo (the Lion) because I never got to know his real name. He lost the lower part of both arms and all of both legs in an accident. I met him at the World Games for physically challenged athletes in Assen, the Netherlands. When I saw Leo, what I experienced was the absolute beauty of his face as well as the way he moved around in a wheelchair. It was breathtaking to watch such grace. If I had not seen it with my own eyes, I wouldn't have believed it possible for him to move like that without any help.

I watched him whenever I could during the games. I was way too shy to speak to him, especially because he was always surrounded by many other athletes. It seemed that a ray of light was with Leo wherever he went. After being around him, people seemed to smile more, laugh more. They joked with him, and he responded with confidence and complete natural ease.

The last night, when we all were celebrating the success of the games, I saw Leo on the dance floor with a paralyzed girl who was also in a wheelchair. He gave her what remained of his arm to hold onto, and off they went, around in circles with such joy that I started to cry out of love.

> *The human brain is hardwired to connect; it is capable of growing new synaptic connections and new neurons through experiences and relationships. It is here we can have our greatest impact.*
>
> DANIEL SIEGEL, MD

spot of grace

I never saw him again, but what he did for my life was to show me that it's possible to overcome life circumstances, no matter how difficult, and live authentically with joy and grace. I think of Leo whenever things in my own life become challenging. His energy will be with me forever. You could say that in seeing his spot of grace, I realized I have one too.

flower

TYLER

JANET SCHAEFFLER • *Detroit, Michigan*

My six-year-old great-nephew, in unique ways, always made me feel like the most important person in the world. He died suddenly a couple years ago, and telling you these little vignettes about him brings him alive again for me.

When Tyler was three, during the intermission of *Disney on Ice*, the little boy behind us dropped a piece of popcorn on the floor. Tyler still had a large box left, and even though he didn't know this child, Tyler took a piece from his own box and gave it to him. I've always used this as an example of a random act of kindness.

If a couple of weeks went by when I didn't see him, he'd greet me with, "It's been a long time since I've seen you. I missed you! I waited and waited and waited." Whenever I arrived at their home, he would immediately take my hand, pull me to the floor with him, and say, "So, what's happening?"

Tyler had an uncanny way of always remembering what was going on in people's lives. About eight months after I had shoulder surgery, long after others had stopped asking, he asked me one day, "Does your shoulder still hurt?"

Filling out a poster about himself in first grade, he completed the sentence, "I wish for . . ." with "everyone in the world to just get along."

Shortly before Christmas, he told his mom and dad, "I don't want

spot of grace

lots of presents this year. I want to get presents and food for the kids who don't have lots of things. I really don't need any more things."

Tyler was truly the most giving, compassionate, sensitive child I've ever known. Each time I said good-bye to him, I left convinced of my worth and wanting to do that for others. Good-bye for now, Tyler.

DAN BENANAV • *Yorktown Heights, New York*

Growing up, I received little attention or affection from my parents. When I was a young teenager my mother, a Holocaust survivor, told me that she had difficulty showing affection because so many of her close relatives, including her parents, had perished. My father, also a Holocaust survivor, was busy working to make ends meet. I never knew anything different, until the day I met Ruth, my older brother's girlfriend at the time, and subsequently his wife.

One of my most vivid and delightful memories is when Ruth read a book to me. As I recall that time, I feel the joy in my heart — the excitement of it — even now, decades later. Like a flower in need of watering, I soaked up the attention. I was seven years old, and until then no one had ever read a book to me. I can still feel the smooth cover, smell the pages, and see the pictures. My whole body smiles when I remember a bike ride we went on. To this day I really enjoy doing dishes, something Ruth and I often did together.

> *The winds of grace are always blowing, but it is you that must raise your sails.*
>
> RABINDRANATH TAGORE

It didn't matter what we were doing; when I was with Ruth I felt special and loved. Everyone needs that, and from that place they can reach out to others in grace. I feel pure gratitude toward Ruth that no words can ever express.

spot of grace

I worked for four years as a teacher with a woman in her sixties whom I'll call Agnes. She was a few inches over four feet tall, had to use a walker, wore sweat suits, and showed up every day with a different-colored wig (she had three) on her otherwise completely bald head. She also loved gaudy costume jewelry and makeup.

When Agnes was growing up, her family considered her mental retardation so shameful that they kept her isolated, locked upstairs in the family home for decades. Agnes was completely deaf and sometimes got very frustrated with not being able to communicate. Since her hands were shaky and she couldn't form many signs, I tried using small picture symbols that she could point to in a book, and within months she was using the book to ask for things and, at her level, talk about her life. When it was break time, for instance, she loved to indicate if she wanted juice, tea, or coffee that day by pointing to the pictures of them. We sewed a cloth bag for carrying the picture-symbol notebook and attached it to her walker or wheelchair. I designed the bag; Agnes cut it out. I pushed the threaded needle into place, and Agnes pulled it through and handed it back to me, until it was done. It opened up the world for her to be able to communicate with other people.

Although Agnes was in her midsixties and severely physically disabled, when I saw her active, engaged body as she clumped down the halls with her walker, I had the idea that she would perhaps like

flower

133

swimming. I took her to the therapeutic, warm swimming pool, but she was clearly distressed at the idea of going in. I began taking her, fully dressed in her wheelchair, to the pool. One day we just sat side by side, watching swimmers and pointing to pictures in her book of "pool" and "swim" and "people." Another time, I brought a cup and let her feel the temperature of the water with her fingers and pour it back into the pool. Bit by bit, over many months, I familiarized her with all the aspects of going swimming. Because she liked pretty clothes and accessories, I bought her a bright, colorful swim cap with big flowers all over it. We made pictures for all the equipment and processes of swimming to add to her book. Finally we got her used to a special wheelchair that could go down the ramp right into the warm water.

On the big day of her first swim, another staff person helped her to change into a swimsuit. Agnes was nervous but I think also excited, and with my arm around her shoulder, we went down the ramp into the toasty water! We celebrated afterward by having coffee together while she pointed to her pictures of each part that she had done. She was clearly proud and showed the "pool" and "Agnes" pictures to several other people that day on her own.

Indian wisdom says our lives are rivers. We are born somewhere small and quiet and we move toward a place we cannot see, but only imagine. Along our journey, people and events flow into us, and we are created of everywhere and everyone we have passed.

LINDA WINGATE

We were over the hump. After about a year, with a life preserver on, she learned to free-float. The peaceful look on her face as she relaxed into floating upright by herself with me three feet away told me that we were giving her something she'd needed for a long time. There was never any doubt in my mind or in Agnes's that grace was alive and well in that pool.

Spending time around people with nonordinary abilities such as mental retardation is a great place to recognize and cultivate your spot of grace and others'. Sometimes it's just like a treasure hunt!

My best friend in the world is named Lillian. She is also the most brilliant person I know (and I know a lot of very smart and special people). Her brain works like no one else's. When we first met I noticed her (how could I not?) because she was dancing alone in the student union of our college wearing a white lab coat to which she'd attached letters spelling out *schizoleptic*. I introduced myself to her and asked what the lab-coat letters meant. "My dad is a paranoid schizophrenic, and my mom is a grand mal epileptic, so I figure I'm a schizoleptic." See what I mean about her original thinking? That was enough for me to become best friends with her for life. A couple years after I moved from West Virginia to San Francisco she followed, and we had many wild adventures together.

I knew that Lillian had had a rough childhood, with her dad institutionalized and her mother working three jobs to support the family. But I did not know about the pain and guilt that had scarred Lillian when she had visited her father in the institution, which sounded like a medieval nightmare. Sometimes Lillian would "go dark." On the rare occasions when she did, the pain and fear of it all came spilling out.

One episode in particular haunted her. It had happened when she, as the oldest daughter, was assigned to visit her father in the institution because the younger children could not handle it. The male patients at the institution had to leave their rooms during the day and wait in the hall of the dank, jail-like ward. They either wandered around like zombies on Thorazine, or they lay down on the cold, hard floor, trying desperately to sleep. When Lillian visited, she said she had to "step over the heads" of the men. "Other people's fathers, too," she added.

After a really bad breakup of a long-term relationship, Lillian started talking more about these visits, so much so that I began referring to them as "head-stepping episodes." She would wail and cry and scream about it while I searched desperately for the right words to say. Suddenly it came to me that role-playing might help. So I lay down on the floor, and we reenacted what had taken place so many years before that had cut Lillian to the quick. As I lay there and Lillian stepped over my head, saying what she used to say to her dad, somehow, some way, I knew exactly what her dad would have wanted to say to her if he had not been medicated to within an inch of his life.

I said the words for him. "I love you so much, Lillian. You are my brave daughter, and I am so proud that you come here to see me. Lots of the other families are too scared to come, but not you. Even though I am in here, I am okay. I had lots of good years with your mom and you when you were little. I will never stop loving you. You are so special to me and my gift to the world."

Lillian's shoulders shook as she cried, walking slowly over me and my imaginary ward mates. That was the last head-stepping episode. Lillian has gone on to become a remarkable success, a hugely talented guitarist and a beloved and excellent teacher. And I learned about what a profound difference we can make when we reach for another with the eternal power of compassion, deep friendship, and love.

flower

DARING TO BE DIFFERENT

PEGGY MEADOR • *Troy, Michigan*

"Mom, I'm different." Many adolescents are confused about their identity or feel self-conscious, but my eleven-year-old daughter has autism, so most of our communication is like solving a puzzle. It takes a while to get to her real concern or feelings about a subject. She has always been sensitive to being rejected on the playground or to people looking at her, but it wasn't until recently that she expressed the feeling that there were kids in this world who look, act, or think differently than she does. It's one of those double-edged swords of autism: my daughter knows there's a difference between her and the general population, and that knowledge can help her to progress or can cause serious depression.

Because she is unable to expound on her thoughts or feelings, I didn't know right away what she meant by "feeling different." Was it that she wears protective ear covers for her sensitive ears? Was it that she rocks when she talks? Was it that she was adopted from Guatemala and has thick, curly, brown hair and black eyes or that she went through an early puberty and has already blossomed into a young woman? Or that she's often grouped with other special-education children rather than her fifth-grade peers?

Sometimes she'll give me a more specific hint at what's bothering her, but trying to tell her that she's exaggerating when she says that "everyone has straight, blond hair except me" only makes her frustrated. And sometimes when she says that her brain is different, she just wants to know that I'm listening. I give her facts about her heritage. I build on her strengths by filling the house with her drawings of wolves and dragons. I tell her she's the best thing that could have ever happened to this family — which she is.

But when Lillian started talking about feeling different, I needed another tool to help her. I decided to teach her a new word: *unique*. I told her that people are not like cars and don't come out of a factory. I explained that everyone is different and each one is an amazing combination and mixture of eye color, hair color, and skin color, with a unique way of thinking and acting and feeling. She was silent for a while, and I didn't know if she understood or could process what I was explaining.

> *The greatest gift of a lifetime is being exactly who you are.*
>
> JOSEPH CAMPBELL

The next day we drove past a park and saw a group of fair-haired children screaming and spinning on a merry-go-round. I noticed from her body language that something about the scene had sparked the "different" feeling again. I prepared to listen with empathy and information, but instead of complaining she just gave me a little smile and said, "Mom, no one's alike; everyone is unique." I sighed in relief, knowing that we can survive autism together, one lesson at a time.

flower

Walking away from five years as a nun is not like leaving a regular job. In 1962, before Vatican II, leaving the convent was seen as losing my vocation, a disgrace. At age twenty-three I carried the added weight of being gay, which was held in check, along with all feelings, by the rule forbidding "particular" friendships. Two Catholic strikes against me. Having to face the larger, unsheltered world felt like the third.

Enter Sybil, a nurse I met while working at my first postconvent job, at Charity Hospital. She invited me out to supper with her roommates, also nurses. They coaxed me into leaving my little garage apartment to live with them. Four lively straight women, with doctors and partying on their minds, and me. I huddled in the back bedroom, weeping over the loss of my life of silence and prayer, the loss of feeling chosen for a closer connection to God, which was the promise of religious life. To their dismay, these kind women could not pull me out of despair.

But Sybil chose to sit with me in my sadness, her easy warmth and affection drawing me out. She held my head in her lap while I cried all five years' worth of tears from held-back emotion, confusion, and self-denial. Sometimes she went in late for her graveyard shift. Any time of the day or night, she would make breakfast or cookies. No matter how long or hard I cried and moaned about wanting to die, Sybil, undaunted by stereotypes of gay women or ex-nuns, stubbornly insisted on naming and befriending my goodness.

When I asked what could I possibly give her in return, Sybil confessed that she felt insecure about writing, never sure of the right grammar or punctuation. In her honeyed Southern accent, she said, "Darlin', teach me how to write!"

I've always loved to write. I've always loved to teach. Both come as easily to me as breathing. In fact, they come so easily that I had never really thought of them as anything special or particularly important. I couldn't, however, refuse Sybil anything. Our lessons did help Sybil with her writing, but they also helped me regain my self-respect and realize that I could make a difference in the world. Sybil saw through my sorrow to who I really was. Because of her caring and clear perception, I could finally claim what was never really lost: my true vocation as a writer and teacher.

flower

TEACHING THROUGH THE FORCE

SEBASTIAN RUTH • *Providence, Rhode Island*

Christian and I had worked together for many years with few musical breakthroughs. Violin was a struggle for him; his autism presented me with the challenge of finding the magical technique that would help him learn. Our lessons had been a process of trying to figure out things he would respond to and then drilling on them for weeks and months.

One day when my typically patient and gentle tone was not doing anything for Christian's interest or attention, I tried something completely different. In the preceding year, we had discovered a common love of *Star Wars*. That first trilogy was an important companion to my childhood — the magical properties of the Force, exciting lightsaber battles, and flying spacecraft all captured my imagination in a powerful way. The second trilogy had been just as important for Christian, and he had brought his *Star Wars* toys to our lessons to share with me. To capture his attention on this day, I said in Yoda's voice, "Padawan, you must concentrate!" He was delighted. He quickly figured out what was going on, and within minutes our lesson was transformed into a dialogue between the Jedi master and the padawan, or apprentice.

Through his intense involvement with *Star Wars*, Christian realized that his growth as a musical learner could be as profound as gaining knowledge and control of the Force. Ever since, I have called him padawan: "Padawan, you must focus your mind and concentrate

spot of grace

142

on the rhythm." Or, "Padawan, you must practice so that you will become a master." And in turn, he responds enthusiastically with, "Yes, Master!"

Star Wars has become more than a theme for our lessons, though. Maria Montessori talked about "sensitive periods" — moments in education when a child's interest in a topic becomes all-consuming. While some educators might try to move a student beyond what they see as a distracting obsession, the Montessori belief is that students will be able to learn everything they need through that topic of fascination. If a child becomes "sensitive" with a particular topic, such as dinosaurs, she or he is allowed to continue pursuing it for several days, weeks, or months beyond the time planned for that unit.

Star Wars is a hot topic for Christian, and he's getting the violin through it. For the Youth Salon this year, he insisted on learning the theme to *Star Wars* on his violin. Over the course of several lessons, I videotaped him with his light sabers, showing off his Jedi skills. For the performance I rented him a set of Jedi robes, and we played the *Star Wars* theme in front of a thirty-foot screen that displayed Christian-as-Jedi, fighting with a light saber.

Christian still struggles with technique, but he has a new grasp of music and the process of becoming a musician. We are continuing together on this life path of the musical Jedi quest. It is as gratifying to me as it is satisfying for him.

The best and most beautiful things in the world cannot be seen or even touched. They must be felt with the heart.

HELEN KELLER

flower

I was offered the opportunity to work in a diversity group for my company. I had attended one diversity course, which I found totally offensive. We were taught that the white male had victimized all of us — minorities, women, each other. Several in the course came close to quitting the company as a result of this experience.

I agreed to help in the diversity program and be on the committee as long as there were no further "victim" courses. The company had received enough complaints that the consultants were fired. New ones were hired who agreed to allow people to think through times they had been respected and times they had been disrespected. All were asked to consider what part they had played in the event and how they had responded or reacted to what had happened.

On the morning of the third day, an African American man in his fifties came early to the class. His eyes were red and swollen. He told me that he had been up all night thinking through what he had learned. He had come to realize that since high school he had thought of himself as a victim and that this belief had tainted everything that came after.

He and his sister were "crossed over" in high school as part of the integration process. They lived in the deep South and were the youngest of fifteen in the family. Every day at school, both of them were spit on, called cruel names, and physically abused. They asked their mother to please let them quit, but she told them that they were part of a movement that was too important to quit and that they had to persevere. His sister had a nervous breakdown, and it was years before she could live a normal life. He thought he had come out of it well — with some anger, a better education, and the opportunity to go to college and get a degree, the only one of his fourteen siblings to do so.

He had a job he loved, a beautiful wife, and two wonderful children. He was a leader in his church and community. What he realized, however, was that every time he had a performance review, or every time one of his children received a lower grade than he felt they deserved, he saw the experience as if he were still in high school, with people still spitting on him and calling him names. He realized he was raising his children to have these same feelings and to see things in the same way.

The night before our conversation, he decided to end this suffering. He said that he knew he needed help to do this, but he also knew he was capable of turning himself around. He asked to be part of the diversity committee so he could help others end their suffering and see themselves as the talented, strong individuals they truly were. He, in fact, went on to do this and became head of the diversity program in the Louisiana office.

That one conversation and the hug and tears that were part of it have stayed with me for years. What a wonderful gift it is to have a few hours and the support necessary to reflect and question ourselves about who we really are, and to be a part of helping others do the same! It is truly a blessing that keeps on rippling and making a difference in many lives.

HOPE EQUALS LIFE

KRISTEN CASHMAN • *Bodega, California*

We sat around a thick mahogany table in a conference room at San Francisco General Hospital, my mother, the social worker, the unsmiling young doctor, and I. Though I don't remember the doctor's exact words, the gist of his message was "There's no hope. Even if your brother came out of the coma, he'd be a vegetable and you'd be spoon-feeding him and wiping his ass for the rest of his life. He's shown no signs of improvement for two weeks and seems to be on the decline. It's time to pull the plug."

I wanted to pound my fists on the table in defiant rage, but instead I calmly shook my head, narrowed my eyes, and turned them away from the doctor. I wanted him out of my sight. He was trying to rob me of the hope I had been clinging to so desperately for the past five weeks, since my brother had fallen out of a window and landed here. Next to me, Mom just sobbed, as though Rik were already dead. I still had faith, but it appeared I was the only one. I knew that my big brother was strong and was still there. It was time for me to look elsewhere for help.

Three days later, I stood beside my brother's bed with Dr. Hui Lin, a traditional Chinese doctor who specialized in brain injuries. He looked at me inquisitively and said, "Very unusual that the sister, not the parents, request my help."

"My brother is my best friend, and he can't die," I said. "Can you help him?"

Dr. Lin looked carefully at Rik — at his scalp stitched up like a baseball, at the tracheotomy tube protruding from his neck, at his yellowed skin and sunken cheeks, at his eyes still unwilling to open, and at his sweaty palms (I knew they were sweaty because I had held them at various times every day for weeks on end). He listened to Rik's weak heartbeat. He turned to me and said in his broken English, "His brain is like apple. Worm has eaten apple. A lot of apple is rotted, but not to core. There is still some life."

I wanted to prostrate myself on the cold linoleum and kiss his feet. Hope! Dr. Lin had hope, the thing that was painfully absent from the face of the young Western doctor, and the most precious resource on the planet to me. Dr. Lin saw what I saw in Rik, the spark of who he was, weaker now than it had been, but still there, still glowing.

Dr. Lin came back the next day to give Rik the first dose of a specially concocted herbal tea. After that I would administer it four times a day through the feeding tube into Rik's stomach.

I got used to hanging the bladders of foul-smelling tea on the IV pole and watching the murky liquid flow into Rik's abdomen as I held his hand. I visualized that I was feeding him life itself.

After a few days of the tea, I thought I could see some color returning to Rik's face, and I was sure he wasn't sweating as much. A week or so later, on a day much like all the others, I was alone in his room. After a feeding, I walked over to the window and stared

flower

vacantly at the blue sky and the courtyard below, sprinkled with emotionally drained family members getting some air and patients taking walks with their IV poles. A boom box and a stack of CDs and tapes sat on the table beside his bed. We had been playing them for him nonstop in the hope that the music he loved so much would help rouse him. The window ledge held an assortment of crystals and other talismans brought by the dozens of friends who had come to visit during the first few weeks but who had all eventually returned to their own lives. The music stopped, so I put on a Grateful Dead bootleg. I turned back to the bed, sat down beside it, and then pleaded to him in my mind, yet again: "Please, Rik. Please wake up."

And then I saw his lips move. In time with the recording, they mouthed the lyric "Going where the wind don't blow so stra-a-a-nge." My heart could have burst. In shock I took his hand and called to him. But there was no response; the single lyric was the only gift I'd get that day. It was more than enough. I wept in gratitude.

A few days after that, one eye opened a crack. Initially, there was no awareness whatsoever behind that eye, but it crept open a bit more each day. Unlike what you see in the movies, Rik didn't wake up all at once. It was a slow process that we weren't even sure was leading anywhere. But soon the other eye cracked open, and eventually he began responding when I asked him to squeeze my hand. The doctors conceded that he was beginning to emerge.

It has been more than twelve years since Rik's accident. He walks with a walker and still falls down a lot; his body trembles, drastically hampering his fine motor skills; his memory is spotty; and his speech is distorted and hard to understand. But he feeds himself and wipes himself and does countless other things on his own. He often cracks jokes, and he can still give me a run for my money at *Jeopardy*. Most important, he's almost always smiling.

His physical limitations preclude his holding a "real" job, but he has built a fulfilling career of volunteer work, helping out at an occupational facility for severely mentally challenged people. I'm sure he brightens their days. He tells me stories about these people, about the grace and joy he finds with them.

Dr. Lin and I knew that Rik's spot of grace hadn't been snuffed out but was still smoldering. It just needed nourishment. For me, those days in the hospital were the darkest of my life, but amid that darkness I managed to stay strong and stand up for my brother. I fought for him, he lived, and since then I've never doubted that hope or I make a difference.

BEING THERE

STEPHANIE RYAN • *Newtown, Connecticut*

I was newly sober and going regularly to AA meetings. Then my mother-in-law, Dolores, died. I was scared because I wasn't crying. How could this be? Dolores had been a most significant teacher to me; in a very real way, she had taught me how to love. My husband and kids were all grief-stricken. What was wrong with me?

At the AA meeting I spoke about my fear of not feeling. After it was over I headed to my car. A huge, scary-looking biker guy, covered in tattoos, approached me. "I heard what you said," he explained. "But what if there is nothing wrong with you? What if your gift is to carry your family over this passageway, to help them grieve?" Then he gave me a huge hug.

After he spoke I realized the truth of his words. I was filled with gratitude: for this softhearted stranger, for the grace of AA, and for myself that I could be there for my family in this way. A few weeks later I had an intense dream about Dolores and sobbed my heart out. I woke feeling peaceful. Grace all around.

spot of grace

IN THE QUAD

ROGER G. JAMES, EDD • *Trinidad, California*

When I was a sophomore in high school, I was in a serious downward spiral. Dark, mysterious happenings in my parents' relationship were creating extreme tension at home. I had little interest in school, learning, sports, or friends. I was starting to use drugs and alcohol to dull the fear and self-loathing I felt. It had always been easy for me to excel in my studies and athletics, but more and more, my success seemed to me unearned and fraudulent. I came to believe that if anyone knew who I really was, they would only confirm how worthless I was.

> *And the day came when the risk to remain a bud was more powerful than the risk to blossom.*
>
> ANAÏS NIN

One day as I was walking across the quad at school, Mrs. Wheeler, one of the guidance counselors, stopped me. "Roger," she said, "I have been looking at your records for the last few years and talking with some of your teachers. I just want you to be aware of the incredible gifts and talents you have been given. Always remember that you can be and do anything you want in this world. It's up to you how you use those gifts."

I had absolutely no idea what to do or say in response to her words. They were so completely contrary to my self-image and self-talk that I wanted to reject them, send them flying back into her mouth. And yet at some level they lodged in me and reverberated in healing ways.

flower

151

I worked hard for many years after that unexpected meeting to embrace and defeat my demons. I experienced a lot of loving support from many people in these struggles. Four decades later, I realize that it was Mrs. Wheeler's single act of affirmation that allowed me to begin the process of recovering and enjoying my goodness, my wholeness. Her kind words truly kindled my desire to contribute my gifts and to receive those of others.

ALL MY DREAMS COME TRUE

LAURIE EASTWOOD • *Park City, Utah*

My sister died of an inoperable brain tumor on December 22, 1996. Her name was Abigail Louise Judd Bishop. She was my younger sister by six years and the baby of the family.

From her diagnosis until her death, she was an inspiration to all who were lucky enough to share that last bit of her life with her. I learned many things from this baby sister, not least of which was the ability to love and embrace life in the face of dire circumstances. She wrote a book about her experience because she wanted to share some insights about her personal journey and use her life to make a difference. She titled it *All My Dreams Came True*.

She often traveled from Utah to California, where I was living at the time, for treatment. We shared so many moments laughing and crying together. Nothing was left unsaid. One day about four weeks before she died, we were sitting on my back terrace and she looked at me and said, "Laurie, if you ever wonder if you've made a difference in the world, know that you have for me." It was the greatest gift I've ever been given because from that moment on, I could never doubt that what I do does, in fact, matter to the world.

flower

THE KIDDOS

TEMPLETON THOMPSON • *Bon Aqua, Tennessee*

I'm a singer-songwriter who's been blessed to combine my two loves, music and horses. For years the horses in my life have been my teachers and my healers. To this day my mare, Jane, and gelding, Beau, continue to teach me what really matters in life: the simple idea of just being alive, being grateful for every single day that I can be here, trying to do the best I can.

I lost a wonderful friend, a fellow lover of horses, and a tender soul who didn't seem to know how wonderful she was. She took her own life just a few days ago. My heart aches for those of us left behind. Very early this morning, I went out to check on the "kiddos," as I call them. There was still a peaceful full moon in the sky, and Jane nickered so low and soft it brought healing tears to my eyes. She was letting me know that my friend is all right and as free as a bird now. She knew what I needed, the way she always does. I promptly went and buried my face in her mane, thanked her for her wisdom, and told her how much I love her and how honored I am to have her and her brother in my life. To all you horse folks out there, here's to our four-legged guardian angels. And to all of you, thanks for listening. Writing down the things that have made such a difference to me has helped heal my aching heart.

JENNIFER CICH • *Ithaca, Nebraska*

We had been married only three years when my husband and I got the news: I had another tumor in my chest cavity. Snuggled between my left lung and heart lay a mass where just six months earlier there had been none. I had been feeling and looking great and had no suspicions that anything was out of the ordinary.

On a Friday afternoon my oncologist showed me the films from the X-rays taken just a few moments before and hugged me. This was the same doctor who, four years earlier, had wrapped his arms around me, a scared twenty-two-year-old student home on spring break to investigate a blockage in her chest. Back then, I had no faith or confidence in the doctor and was terrified of what the future held for me, but that soon changed. When I was a patient in the hospital, Doc came to my bedside after visiting hours, even if he wasn't on rounds, to check on me. We talked about the personal effects of cancer and how limiting — but at the same time how freeing — it can be. I was a crybaby, but the doctor was a rock through my treatments. Each visit he would take extra time with me, tell me I was beautiful, give me one of those warm, strong hugs for support, and walk me through what we could expect this round.

As we cleared sixty-three treatments and radiation and moved into the realm of remission, our appointments dwindled. Then came the appointment that showed the second tumor. Surprisingly, I wasn't angry, upset, or scared when he gave me what should have

flower

155

been devastating news since I was a young woman looking to start a family. I remembered the talks the doctor and I had had four years earlier — how cancer patients must be like frogs, always hopping forward, never looking backward, always singing, especially in the rain. I looked to the new diagnosis as another gift, an opportunity to grow deeper in faith, family, and love.

I completed the second round of twelve one-week treatments, stem cell transplants, and radiation three years ago and saw my doctor for a checkup last week. I had my mom by my side when the doctor came into the room. With a somber expression, saying nothing, he made a beeline for my chair and enveloped me in his arms. All I could think was, "Here we go again!" Instantly I prepared myself for the words I didn't want to hear. The doctor held me at arm's length and looked into my eyes, smiling softly. "Everything looks great. I'm just so glad to see you. I've missed my old friend."

> *In order to understand what another person is saying, you must assume it is true, and try to imagine what it could be true of.*
>
> GEORGE MILLER

I thanked Doc for his courage, strength, and commitment to support me as I made the decisions that enabled me to grow through the experience. I wonder how different the outcome would have been if he hadn't been my caregiver, opening himself to me from his shining spot of grace. Today I carry that shine with me, and I share it with as many people as possible.

GOLGOTHA

ADKE VAN KUIJK • *Alkmaar, the Netherlands*

Some years ago we were staying at our family chalet in Belgium. The house overlooks a beautiful valley, with several hills in the distance. I had been going through a time of great inner pain and sadness, realizing that my mother never wanted me to be born and thus never received or loved me the way I needed.

One morning the sky was rather peculiar, totally gray without clouds or wind. Looking out the window, I suddenly saw three perfectly vertical beams of light. The middle one was the broadest and highest. The ones on either side were perfectly symmetrical. Because the beams appeared over a hilltop, the image of Golgotha rose strongly in my mind. After a short while, the beams began to drift away very slowly. Then they tilted and dissolved.

The whole scene felt very comforting, as if I had been told to stop crucifying myself with the story that I should not be alive. I realized in that instant that I do matter, whether people demonstrate their love for me or not. The strange thing was that my husband, Peter, didn't notice the beams of light. He was sitting with his back to the window, and apparently I didn't tell him to turn around.

It would be nice if I could say that from then on I was "enlightened," but this was not the case. However, that experience, that moment, was and is a great help to me in learning to love life and myself unconditionally. More and more, I grow to understand that life is primarily about accepting things the way they are, even with slowly

flower

diminishing or, better yet, changing possibilities caused by multiple sclerosis.

I experience more and more that I am not a victim of other people or circumstances. If I make the choice, I can use all of it to learn that my happiness is independent of favorable or unfavorable events. I can create my own life and happiness.

I must say that I am now much happier than I was when I was still healthy. Being victimized is all about fear. When fear diminishes, life becomes very worthwhile!

UNCONDITIONAL RECIPROCITY

DIANE GROFF • *Denver, Colorado*

I have a friend named Joan. She does not know that she has given me the most incredible gift. She is dying now. She cannot speak anymore, but her eyes and her little smile speak volumes. Words are not needed; a touch, a smile, a gaze, holding hands all communicate caring, support, and unconditional love. She receives the love I send her and acknowledges it in her own way.

Joan is teaching me that it is a gift to just be with someone, to give love unconditionally, freely, just because my heart and soul want to, not because I will receive anything back in the usual manner. I receive so much more, at a deeper soul level, just being in her presence and giving my presence. Some deep exchange of knowing and feeling transcends our usual forms of communication.

When I had cancer Joan was at my side during chemo treatments, and I was blessed by her loving care and comfort. Now as I reach back to her, she is teaching me about the amazing gift of unconditional love. Thank you, my friend, for helping me find the courage to share this gift with others, for both of us.

flower

fruit

Who Stands in Front of You?

It is from numberless diverse acts of courage and belief that human history is shaped. Each time a person stands up for an ideal, or acts to improve the lot of others, or strikes out against injustice, he or she sends forth a tiny ripple of hope, and crossing each other from a million different centers of energy and daring, those ripples build a current that can sweep down the mightiest of walls of oppression and resistance.

ROBERT F. KENNEDY, *"Day of Affirmation" speech, University of Cape Town, South Africa*

My parents never found a way to explain death to me, but my grandmother did. My beloved Aunt Chuch had just died in our house. As I watched my grandmother braid golden dough for the Sabbath bread, I asked where people go when they die and if they ever come back again. Rather than answering me, she tore a long strip from the newspaper that had been covering the table. Her gnarled, nimble fingers turned the ends toward each other as if to make a circle but then made one twist in the strip and joined the ends together with a sticky dab of dough. She didn't know it was called a Möbius strip, but Grandma understood things from a place deeper than words.

She took my chubby finger and traced it around the outside of the loop, whispering as she always did to indicate that a mysterious secret was about to emerge.

"When Chuch was alive, she lived here, on the outside, but when she died . . ." Her floury hand guided my finger through the place she

fruit

had twisted, the turning point. To my great surprise, my finger now was moving around the inside of the loop.

She continued, "When Chuch died, she moved here, inside of your heart. But each time you tell a story about her..." Once again she moved my finger through the turning place, until it was tracing the outside of the loop again. "...This story will bring her alive for you and anyone who hears it. That's why telling stories is important, *ketʒaleh*. They make it possible for whatever has been most precious to come alive again and again."

Then, as now, my mind was composed of endless ribbons of questions that seemed to annoy most grown-ups but not my grandmother. "How does Aunt Chuch get inside? And does everybody die? Will I lose everybody?"

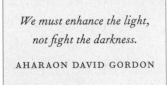

We must enhance the light, not fight the darkness.

AHARAON DAVID GORDON

She slid me up on her aproned lap and began to rock slowly back and forth, back and forth. This always slowed the questions long enough for her to respond.

"Being human, *ketʒaleh*, means that someday we will lose everyone and everything. But, here..." Her warm hand came to rest on the center of my chest. "Here, there is this island in your heart. Everyone has one," she said, "but most people forget when they grow up. Someday each of us loses everything that's precious to us, at least on the outside. That's just the way life is meant to be. But what is on the island is ours to keep forever. So it's important, very important, to really enjoy what we love, to memorize it and absorb it so deeply into you that it will take root on the island."

"What happens to the island when I die, Grandma? Does it go with me?"

Pressing her wrinkled cheek against my fuzzy one, she nodded and whispered. "But of course, *ketzaleh*. Of course. So memorize these moments like you do your spelling words. Memorize them well."

For some kids, being in school is the best six hours of the day. They get one or two good (well, decent, anyhow) meals a day, they get to hang out with their friends, they maybe learn something interesting, and they're safe. No strangers walking into the house, no "uncle" or cousin suddenly arrested or worse. In my first year of teaching, I learned that such kids can get something even more important.

Rasheem would come to my classroom during his lunchtime. He was a loner but not lonely. His mother worked two hours away from home. It was a single-parent family. He had a twenty-three-year-old brother who worked nights and was almost always sleeping when Rasheem was awake. I was told Rasheem had an undefined learning disability and saw things as a quarter of the size they really were.

At first all we did was sit and talk. Then, when I ran out of things to say about PlayStation 2, I took out a deck of cards and taught him to play gin rummy. He became a gin rummy fanatic. He looked at the clock during our slowly expiring half hour and figured out how many hands we had left before the bell rang. And he talked to the cards. When he picked one from the deck he would say, "Ah, maybe." When he was looking to discard, he'd talk to it as if talking to an old toy: "Well, I thought I needed you, but I guess not."

I usually gave him half of my sandwich. He asked me, "Can't you eat a whole sub?" And I said, "Yeah, but really, it's more fun to share." He said, "I know," and looking at the clock, he said, "Eight minutes. Time for — at least — two more hands."

What I learned in my first year of teaching with Rasheem is that school and teachers must offer something unconditional: faith. Faith that the student, no matter how awful, rude, or vulgar he may have acted on Monday, can be entirely redeemed by his behavior on Tuesday. We've got 180 days a year to hope they can learn to grow that faith in themselves.

MY BROTHER, THE OTHER[*]

JEAN FERACA • *Madison, Wisconsin*

The dedication of my book reads, "In memory of my brother, Stephen, for all his othering." There was nobody like my brother. He reached out to people far beyond our ken and gathered them into his tribe: people like Stephen Lohr, his brilliant wheelchair-bound friend who was stricken with cystic fibrosis; Louie Mofse, his Indian friend who could dance with sixteen hoops; and Mary Fast Horse, his adopted Sioux mother, a wise and saintly old woman. Because of his unique gifts, he taught me to recognize my own giftedness. His love for people and expansive worldview became the template for the work I now do as the host of *Here on Earth: Radio Without Borders*, a public radio program premised on the idea that there is only one race — the one we call human.

My brother Stephen died of lung cancer on June 29, the feast of St. Peter and St. Paul. To watch somebody with a life force that verged on the diabolic reduced to a box of ashes overnight was a shock. I'm grieving.

He had started smoking at the age of eleven. Butts he picked up in the street. Unfiltered Pall Malls. Then regular Chesterfields. And finally, Marlboros, which he consumed two or three packs at a time. He never stopped. Not even after throat cancer and two operations. He was deeply addicted.

spot of grace

---

[*] Excerpted from "My Brother/The Other," in *I Hear Voices: A Memoir of Love, Death, and the Radio*.

Ours was an Italian-American family rooted in the Bronx, but for some mysterious reason, Stephen became completely identified with Indians from the moment my mother showed him a picture of a Plains Indian warrior on horseback when he was five. As my brother got older, his psyche became a battleground where the Indian Wars were never settled.

He became more and more difficult as he grew older, flying off the handle at the slightest provocation. We learned to live with him the way the Neapolitans live with Vesuvius, never knowing from one minute to the next just when he might blow. He was a living contradiction. Whatever could be said of him, the opposite was also true. He was kind-hearted, but he could be equally cruel; he had the manners of a courtier when he wanted to be charming, downright gallant one minute, shockingly crude the next. He was a romantic and a cynic, a skeptic and a true believer. His knowledge of the history of North American Indians was encyclopedic; he was trained as an anthropologist in the scientific method, but, underneath it all, he practiced magic.

He worshipped Crazy Horse and Sitting Bull, Lorenzo de Medici and Mussolini; he preached benign dictatorship, and practiced a form of petty tyranny at home. "He was never any good at anything that mattered," his daughter once said of him. "A great artifaker," was what he called himself, speaking of his uncanny ability to recreate Indian artifacts, but really the same was true of his own makeup. Only a very few of us could see through his bluff. "Steve is like America," his friend Cesare said. "Love him or leave him." His wife left him. His children left him. But I always adored him, and so did my two sons.

He was my big brother by ten years, always defending and protecting me in family quarrels and street scuffles. When I was a kid, he carved me a child's bow and arrows from ash tree saplings he had cut down in Van Cortland Park. Yippee, his hunting dog, an English fox terrier, very smart, used to follow him into the park to hunt rabbits and squirrels. He taught me to shoot into the bull's-eye of a target he nailed into one of the oak trees in our backyard in Riverdale. He taught me how to do the deer dance and insisted that I practice every day when I came home from school, running upstairs to his room to seek him out. There was an alcove attached to his bedroom where I used to love to hang out. It was chock-full of all kinds of fascinating things that were always kept in meticulous order: comic books, Chinese coins, drawing pencils, flints and arrowheads and rabbits' feet. He was a tough and exacting first teacher who instilled in me the same standards of excellence to which he himself scrupulously adhered.

We performed in minstrel shows together. While he beat out the rhythm on one of his hand-stretched drums and sang in a high nasal voice, Indian style, I danced the deer dance, all decked out as an Indian brave in a costume he had conjured out of ribbons, beads, and turkey feathers. The last thing he did before each performance was to tie a headband around my head and paint each of my cheeks with two yellow streaks and one red dot. I wore a breechcloth, a vest, and a turkey feather bustle he helped me fix around my waist. I was supposed to shake a rattle in my right hand while fluttering a turkey feather fan in the left. That took some doing. I don't think I ever got it right. Best of all were the real beaded buckskin moccasins Chief Hill Canoe had made just for me that I wore with strings of bells around my ankles so that whenever I moved, I jingled. We performed this brother-and-sister act many times together on stages and auditoriums throughout the Bronx until I finally got too big to be passed off as an Indian brave.

What a lucky bastard he was, when I think about it. To live your whole life a prodigal and a reprobate only to die like a saint. He really did look like one of the desert fathers when we walked into his hospital room and found him swaddled in nothing but a sweaty sheet. He had always been afraid he would die alone. He had been disinherited by my father after a terrible quarrel. Stephen hadn't come to my father's funeral. That was a disgrace. Ten years went by when none of us talked to him, not even me. Yet there he was, surrounded by his tribe: sisters, daughter, sons, lovers, friends of every hue and stripe, his family reunited, even Jo Anne, his gentle ex-wife.

I remember how he had hooked a rug from nails on a spool when he was a boy, lifting off the thread from each nail head until the hank grew to a fantastic length, a quarter mile or more, as the story was told. And here he was, hooking the rug of his life off the spool one stitch at a time while the hank went on disappearing slowly down the hole. I had never before realized how each of us has just so many breaths, a finite number, an allotment assigned to us like the number you get in a bakery or a butcher's shop. And the more we use them up, the more each one of these breaths becomes a thing unto itself, discreet as a shaped note. In . . . out . . . in . . . out . . . all through his last night on earth. Nothing to suggest that the end was near. No faltering. No stumble. No slowing down at all. And then it stopped. I felt like a diver who had just let go of the boat. I looked at the clock. Ten

fruit

171

minutes to six. He took one last half breath. When the nurse came in she was just as surprised as we were that the end had come. She checked his pulse, looked up at us and said, "He was a brilliant warrior."

My son Dominick shaved him. Together, we removed his hospital gown. I washed his hands and feet, taking liberties with my brother's body I never would have dreamed of taking while he was alive. All the while, he was giving off heat in waves that kept rising off his forehead as if it were coming up from some deep source, like coal compressed under many layers, buried in his core. His heat was purgative, erasing all traces of the anguish and torment that had characterized his last days, his whole life, in fact. In their place, a deep peace came to settle into him like a great stone that had finally found its groove. It seemed to suggest that his suffering, the very cruciform of his life, had been redemptive after all. The work was unfinished, but the man was complete.

SECRET AGENT

NANCY MARGULIES • *Montara, California*

In August of 1998, boarding a Greyhound bus heading from Boulder to Denver, I noticed a young black woman standing in line. I'd been in Aspen, and she was the first black person I had seen in a week. As we climbed on, she noticed the silver bracelet I was wearing.

"I like your bracelet," she said.

"Thanks. I bought it in Mexico recently," I explained.

She told me that this thin silver chain was just the type of bracelet she'd been looking for. I offered to give her mine.

> *While we have the gift of life, it seems to me the only tragedy is to allow part of us to die — whether it is our spirit, our creativity, or our glorious uniqueness.*
>
> GILDA RADNER

"Oh, no, I couldn't" was her immediate response.

"It's okay," I reassured her. "It wasn't expensive."

"Maybe I can buy it from you," she suggested.

"Look," I said, "what would be more fun — buying a bracelet from a total stranger or receiving a gift from a total stranger?"

She admitted that the gift would be much better. I took the bracelet off my wrist and put it on hers. It looked great. We found seats, one behind the other, and there was no more conversation. Leaving the bus, the young woman handed me a piece of notebook paper folded several times into a neat square. I

fruit

thanked her and stuck it in my back pocket. A few hours later I remembered the paper and read it. In pencil she had written:

Dear Miss:

Today was an important day for me. You see, I am going out into the world without the protection of my family to see what it is like. Soon I will be going off to college, and today I am trying out being on my own away from home. Thank you so much for being the first person I was to meet.

God bless.

A. Stranger

I have her note framed on my wall. One of my favorite possessions. Perhaps I was born to welcome that young woman into the world of strangers. I may have been sent to Denver that day not to see my sister but to meet that one person on the bus. I'll never know. But from that meeting on, I was clear that the best way for me to live is to treat every event, each stranger, as a potential opportunity to act as an agent of the divine.

TRAVELING MERCY

SANDY RHYASON • *White Rock, British Columbia*

I was a Handidart driver, providing transit for anyone unable to travel on regular transportation, for over thirteen years. It might not seem like much of a job, but because of one old man, I learned that I can really make a difference.

Mr. Fraser lived alone, as his wife of sixty-two years was now in a nursing home. Each time I picked him up to drive him to see his wife, he would carefully push his walker out to the van, balancing a treasure of baked goods that he faithfully brought to her. Each week he instructed me to be careful with his package.

> *Just as despair can come to one only from other human beings, hope, too, can be given to one only by other human beings.*
>
> ELIE WIESEL

One particular trip, I could see that Mr. Fraser was feeling pretty down. He spoke about how lonely he was and how unfair life is. Wanting to somehow cheer him up, I asked him to tell me about his wife. He looked at me like he had no idea what I was talking about. I primed the pump by asking him how old Mrs. Fraser was when they first started dating. That was all it took. As memories flooded back into his mind, he told me all about his precious wife, describing what a terrific wife she had been to him all through their marriage. When we arrived, I carefully set up his walker and gently set his treat for his wife on top. Mr. Fraser turned to me, our eyes met, and our souls touched.

fruit

"Thank you," he said slowly. I could tell he wasn't too sure exactly what had just happened, but he did know he was about to enjoy a wonderful visit with his sweetheart. I felt privileged to have been his driver, and I am forever grateful that the universe brought us together that day to share one moment of grace that began with a simple question asked in wonder and ended with a sense of what really matters.

YOU AIN'T GONNA MAKE ME READ*

DAWNA MARKOVA

I had been hired as a learning specialist in a migrant labor camp in Florida, which meant keeping the kids no one else could teach out of trouble. My office was a small, dark room that was also the janitor's supply closet. It was Jerome who broke me open. He was fifteen, in fifth grade, twice as big as I was, and labeled as being too retarded to learn to read and too disruptive to be with other kids. The first thing he said to me was, "You ain't gonna make me read." Hey, I wasn't stupid. This kid had fists bigger than my purse. It was clear I wasn't going to *make* him do anything. I did what I learned from my grandmother. I searched for the spot of grace in his soul.

It's really nothing more complicated than the act of noticing and cherishing. In Jerome's case, I noticed that he was anything but empty or stupid. He was the chess champion of the migrant labor camp. He played brilliantly. No matter who his opponent was, he shone. The chessboard was his natural field of mastery, and it became obvious that all I needed to do was find the bridge between what he knew about playing chess and learning to read.

What motivated Jerome to play was the challenge of the game. So I left a thick book with lots of photographs and gold letters, *A History of Black America*, on my desk and bet him that if we played a game of chess and I won, he would learn to read it. If he won, I would

fruit

---

* Excerpted and adapted from *I Will Not Die an Unlived Life: Reclaiming Purpose and Passion*.

read it to him. Knowing I was seriously remedial in the game, he took the bet. With divine intervention, I won (the one and only time I have ever won a game of chess!). I taught him to read the way he played chess — through his body, then his eyes, and in silence. In a few short months he went from being a "retarded illiterate" to a shining and obsessive reader. He taught me that people have many ways of processing information, many learning patterns, instead of only one, as I had been taught in education classes. From this insight sprouted my life's work in intellectual diversity, which I've researched, taught, and written about for forty-five years.

Jerome never became an A student. Chances are that he dropped out of school. Chances are that he's either in a prison or dead by now. But whether in a cell or heaven, I'd be willing to bet that he's still reading and that he knows he's not dumb.

LIBERATING WHAT CAN BE POSSIBLE

MARTINE CARALY • *Strasbourg, France*

Sometimes it is only in fighting for what really matters to us that we can recognize that we really matter. Yahyia is a sturdy, short, forty-year-old man. Almost everything about him is dark — hair, eyes, complexion. His bright white teeth light up his face when he smiles. His fierce mustache travels wildly bottom up, almost reaching his bushy, black brows, a flag announcing his joy. His eyes shine like two dark marbles: he is alive and kicking, making up for his height by standing very erect, stretching his spine to gain a few inches. Yahyia is a man of honor, a Kurdish national with a wife, nine children, acres of agricultural land, and many cattle. He is rich in his community, which is bordered by both Turkey and Iraq.

Yahyia is also a man of vision and peace. He participated in the general election, advocating reconciliation between the Kurds and the Turks. In a country where freedom of speech and belief is a crime, he was beaten up, his family was threatened, and their dog was killed in front of his terrified children. He was dragged down the dusty road in front of his house, thrown in a cell, beaten and tortured, and then thrown out again and told to disappear.

He paid every cent he had to be smuggled in the undercarriage of a truck to France. He had no idea when he would see his wife and children again. On the way he was dumped somewhere in frozen Germany. He had no more money to continue the journey, so he slaved away until he had enough to resume the trip. Then he was

fruit

179

brutally arrested on the border, in Strasbourg. He managed to escape and went into hiding.

Without knowing anything about him, I hired him to work on the construction of my house. Because I speak several languages, including Arabic, I could unravel the strands of his story. When my house was finished, Yahyia was hired to build the new police headquarters. His identity became known as he finished this work, and he was sent to a cell and waited to be removed from the French territory as an illegal resident. He had applied for papers, asking for asylum status, showing the scars of torture on his body as proof. The status was refused, and he was sentenced to be returned to his own country. This was as good as a death penalty. Both my sons (fifteen and twelve), who had gotten to know Yahyia when he worked on our house, and I could not accept this.

We started the fight with just the three of us, visiting Yahyia daily in his cell at the retention center. He got bonier and grayer by the day. The shine in his eyes disappeared. Even his mustache drooped. Everything about him seemed to be falling downward. Life was leaking out of him as hope and dignity were replaced by a grim fear and grief. My kids and I were all alone, and it seemed impossible that we could make a difference, but not doing anything was unfathomable. We threw ourselves in the battle. As people heard about what we were doing, they came to support us. Their numbers grew quickly. We even got inside information from prison wardens that helped us in the legal process.

I will not dwell on the many miracles that occurred. The day he was to leave in a plane to be turned over to his former tormentors was also my birthday. One of my friends was the diva performing at the National Opera House. To my complete surprise, Yahyia was her guest of honor, seated next to a high government official. It was the best gift I could ever dream of getting. He and all his fellow inmates had been released.

In moments now when I stumble in a dark corner, I think of that shining memory, and it gives me the light I need to keep fighting for those who must be freed. My own sense of what I can make possible was liberated with this man.

WILHELM WEINER, PHD. • *Brooklyn, New York*

It was March 13, 1938. Hitler marched into Vienna, Austria. He was greeted by ecstatic crowds, frenzied in their applause. His parade of swastikas swam in the air like birds bringing unknown fruits of deliverance. Everyone was out except the Jews. We were hiding in our apartments, trembling with fear, aware that his entrance meant possible extermination for not wearing the swastika and thus being recognized as what Hitler had described as "the enemy, the crud of the earth who had betrayed all that Germany and its allies stood for." He proclaimed that, "Only total removal could re-create the world as it was meant to be."

My family and I, in our soon-to-be-destroyed apartment, were living among both Christians and Jews. There were five of us: mother and father, I and a younger brother in our midteens, and our eight-year-old brother. Our building superintendent, Fritz, was Christian. How would we be dealt with? Who would be allowed to live, who destined to perish? Fritz was key. He would be asked the crucial question: "Where are the Jews?"

That day arrived. "Are there Jews living in this building?" asked the Nazi youth in their impeccable uniforms and emotionless voices, as though they were asking if there were mice or roaches in the basement. Looking directly at them, shoulders square, voice simple and strong, Fritz replied without mincing words. "No Jews here. Only Christians."

In the days that followed, Fritz behaved as he always had in his role as superintendent of the building. Occasionally he asked if we were well, if we needed anything. The Nazi storm troopers filled the streets, shooting at random anyone they wished — a child stealing potatoes for starving Jewish parents, a young man with a Jewish star sewn on his arm — then laughing as if they were at an amusement park shooting at duck decoys.

Ah, Fritz, how you must have loved humanity to take such a risk! I wonder if you knew you saved these five lives. I know that all who did not have supers like you — most of my extended family — were slaughtered in their homes or in the camps.

We stayed, living as though at any moment our lives could be cut off with the snap of a finger. Finally, in August of 1939, we left. War broke out the next month. We went to America, living at first with an aunt who had migrated to the States some years earlier when she foresaw what was to come. I grew up determined to honor Fritz's love of humanity and grow it in myself. Perhaps it was part of the reason I decided to become a psychotherapist and psychoanalyst and in that small way serve others.

Fritz was an ordinary human being, but he acted with pure consciousness and connection in the most superior of ways. He was just a super. He was also a just and superior being.

TUCKING IN TIGERS

SARAH MARTINEZ-HELFMAN • *Haverford, Pennsylvania*

The adolescent boys from the residential treatment center were on their way either to jail or back into the community. I was the chief clinician and decided to take them camping. The afternoon we set out, I ventured into the woods with three of the boys. Before long, we had linked elbows, chanting, "Lions and tigers and bears, oh, my!" One of the boys leaned close and whispered, "If you tell anyone about this, I'll kill you," and though he was smiling, I didn't doubt that he meant it.

That night I played guitar and sang to the teens as darkness settled around us. Eventually I went from sleeping bag to sleeping bag, asking each boy if he wanted to be tucked in. The youngest, a guarded thirteen-year-old who made everything into a joke to protect himself, nodded at my offer. I pulled the opening of the bag to his chin and kissed his forehead. He started to cry, saying he'd never been tucked in before. That was all it took. Right then, I knew that I mattered.

> *I am only one, but I am still one. I cannot do everything, but still I can do something. I will not refuse to do the something I can do.*
>
> HELEN KELLER

spot of grace

I never named it as such, but I have always known everyone has a spot of grace. My purpose in life is to be present for the children of the world and help them become who they were born to be. I never thought about this as my own unique gift until Ben came into my life.

Twenty-three years ago, I was struggling with rheumatoid arthritis, just trying to make it through the days taking care of buildings and doing housework whenever I could. A young couple expecting their first child asked me to help them with child care because I had been a teacher. Ben arrived, and right from Day One I knew he was gifted. That didn't mean he was easy to care for.

By the time he was three, I was telling him to let his mother win some of the daily battles. She did not want to let a male, not even her son, get the better of her. She kept looking for what was wrong with Ben. To this day, I can hear him asking me what they would try and fix next. It still hurts me to remember that. I bought books for his mother to read about children, hoping she would learn to see the special child I saw. He went through school labeled a special-ed child. I knew he was special, but not in the same way they meant it. He was an eagle in a chicken coop.

When Ben was a senior in high school, he volunteered at a Jesuit retirement home. He told me that I had always made him feel special, and that experience gave him the chance to make others feel special too. When he had to write an autobiography that year, he

fruit

185

mentioned me as the person in his life who loved him for who he was. I keep his pages in my prayer book.

Ben just graduated from Clark University. I know he can fly. I am sixty-eight years old now, and it feels good to be able to accept that I too am special in my own way because I made a difference in Ben's life.

THE FIRST NAMING AND THE SECOND GIFT

BARBARA PARMET • *Santa Barbara, California*

Old Mrs. R. lived alone across the street. Her husband, who had been a world-famous poet, was long dead. I don't remember seeing anyone ever come or go from her house. I do remember having small neighborly chats. She was lonely, and occasionally we found excuses to stop and speak to each other. One day I was dancing in my living room when she came to the door. I was out of breath and a bit embarrassed. I had on one of my gypsy skirts and had been belly dancing with abandon. She asked me if I could move a box of books for her. It was an ordinary and simple interaction. As I was leaving after moving the box, she said, apropos of nothing I had told her about myself, "It is so wonderful that you are a poet." I smiled and waved as I walked back across the street. Little did she know how ecstatic I was that she had pronounced me a poet.

Mrs. R. died soon thereafter. Now, thirty years later, I think of her and am still grateful for the royal title she bestowed upon me. I had always been and will always be a poet. She was the first to see and name my gift.

Although my two brothers, my parents, and I have always exhibited strong opinions and been fearless in making our voices heard, I can think of no time growing up when there were tender words or gentle hugs. Anger and forgiveness alternated in the form of jokes and laughter. The unspoken code in my family was if you could laugh, all

fruit

problems were solved. Thus, after one of my tearful breakdowns, my father was sent up to my room to tell me a joke until I finally smiled. Then, exit stage left. And so I grew up strong with a sense of humor, capable of arming myself against the world's cruelties.

In 1989, after making some life-sized photographic portraits of two seemingly healthy men with the HIV virus for a "Window on AIDS" community art project in Santa Barbara, I found that my old psychological armor was no longer capable of saving me from rage and sadness. It was a time when coming out as gay in the community was still taboo, especially because of the link to AIDS. Before it was generally known how HIV was transmitted, family members and friends often disowned their sons and lovers and best friends out of fear of catching the "plague." Any informed person knew the disease was blood borne and not easily transmitted. And yet the fear remained. I was outraged by the outcast status of all these dying people. For me, it seemed exactly like how the Nazis treated the Jews — as if they were wild, rabid animals that should be destroyed.

> *When inspired by a grand purpose, a wonderful project, your thoughts shatter their bonds; your mind travels beyond limitations; your consciousness extends in all directions; and you discover a new and amazing world. Hidden forces, talents and faculties spring to life and you find yourself to be far greater than you ever dreamed you could be.*
>
> PATANJALI

When Dan and Dave (the two lovers I had photographed) started a group for others with HIV, they called the organization Helping Hand. We drove people to doctors' appointments and support groups.

I'll never forget the time a vanload of us went down to Los Angeles to hear a powerful and loving woman speak at an AIDS fundraising event. She made two thousand sad, raging, and dying people stand up and cry and hug and be grateful for their precious lives. We drove back to Santa Barbara, and when I got out of the van, Dan came up to me and gave me the most loving, tender hug I had ever received in my life. He told me he loved me.

Six months later, Dan was dead. Through the magic of a prerecorded tape, he sang at his own funeral, his voice soaring through the spacious cathedral. The unconditional love he gave was the spark necessary to transform my rage into the kind of compassion that is capable of comforting those facing death. I have since cultivated that sacred spark, and I treasure the fearlessness that Dan ignited in the world.

The look is instantly recognizable: a slight bit of disarray, a slouched shoulder, and a frantic eye searching for a remedy.

Recently, my son and I were returning home from our first mother-son trip since the twins were born. We couldn't have had a better time. We had arrived at the airport on time and were headed to security with our backpacks. I was gloating because traveling with one child was light-years easier than with three. We were floating along without a care in the world when suddenly a woman just ahead of us caught my attention.

Her eyes were the giveaway — red, swollen, and still teary. I had noticed her earlier, sitting in the terminal next to a man and a baby in a stroller. But here she was in front us now, without the man. And the baby was fussing. There were bags everywhere — diaper bag, clothing bag, bottles in a bag — all attached to her or the stroller in awkward ways. Her eyes met mine, and I froze. She needed me.

"Are you okay?" I asked quietly as I put my hand on her shoulder. She looked at me in disbelief. Then relief.

"What can I do?" She looked baffled. I sprang into action, directing my son to start grabbing bags. "You get your baby, and we'll get the rest," I ordered. We functioned as if we were a NASCAR pit crew. We unfolded the stroller and had her back together in no time.

My spirits sank, though, as I watched a female security agent approach and ask to check her bags. The agent began to rifle through her things. Oh, my poor new friend. Could she bear it? My uncertainty quickly receded when I heard the agent say, "Oh, honey, let me help you get organized." I knew that I had handed her off to another compassionate mother, and my job was done. I went to her to say good-bye and reassure her that she'd be fine now. She was still tearful, but her smile said enough. We turned and walked away.

As we headed to our gate, my son asked why we had helped her. My answer was simple. We helped her because she needed it. We did it because it is right to recycle the goodness that we receive in our own lives. Whether he understood did not matter to me. What was important was that I felt privileged to have the opportunity to pass the goodness on.

It is sometimes hard to describe, even to myself, what being a mother means, but I'd like to think that it includes the capacity to act unselfishly in an instant. I walk just a little bit straighter now, as if there is starch in my backbone, even with diaper bags on my back and a young one on my hip. It is as if that day in the airport, I reclaimed my own dignity as a woman and mother, knowing that I can make a significant difference to other people in very ordinary ways.

fruit

WARRIORS OF LIGHT

CARMEN FREEMAN • *Arvada, Colorado*

In the late 1980s I attended a gathering of women held in the forts around San Francisco. The women were there so they could be with other women, share stories and music, and seek healing. The gathering offered information, emotions, sounds, food, and rituals. We departed completely spent. I rested the whole next day to recover from the intensity of the experience.

I never forgot my time with those women, and in late 1987, after moving to Boulder, Colorado, I began having visions about a gathering that I was to create. It was to be a national retreat, populated by all types of African American women, held in spa-like settings and on reservations.

After my daily spiritual practice, I would often "see" various elements that needed to be incorporated in this new type of gathering to empower, heal, and connect the women who would come. In 1989 I began articulating the vision and was blessed with a response from a dynamic, diverse group of women who became the Warriors' Steering Committee. Together, in 1990, we created the retreat series "Women of Color as Warriors of Light."

We were joined by renowned celebrities and community leaders from various states as well as massage therapists, writers, mothers, grandmothers, lawyers, doctors, artists, organizers, and even street people, from nine years of age to ninety. We said to the women, "We are calling you." They responded to our call.

We always began in Sacred Circle, an environment of safety, and introduced ourselves to each other by answering a significant question, such as, "Who do you currently perceive yourself to be, and what gifts do you bring to this gathering?" It was enchanting to observe the healing begin in the very first moments, when someone would be profoundly affected by this question.

After returning home, many women felt empowered to actualize their dreams. The retreats served as a catalyst for the career of a previous "closet" artist who is now well known for her work with quilts and community art. It empowered women to create or broaden careers, improve their relationships, discuss and reframe the effects of rape and violence, embrace their spirituality, and strive for financial freedom. We encouraged the participants to go back to their various states and communities and "infect others" with their fire. The gatherings ended in 1999. Throughout their history, these women warriors of light recognized the spots of grace in themselves and mentored many others all over the country to do the same.

> *Love is a high inducement for the individual to ripen, to become world, to become world for oneself and for another's sake. It is a great exacting claim upon you, something that chooses you out and calls you to vast things.*
>
> RAINER MARIA RILKE

fruit

PAY ATTENTION TO WHAT YOU LOVE

SUE CROSS • *Arlington, Massachusetts*

The first person to help me recognize that I was unique was my Hungarian maternal grandmother, or nagymama (pronounced "nudge-mama"). What I remember most about my nagymama was the gentle touch of her soft, wrinkled hands.

Nagymama's love was handmade. When we visited, she would wake me up early in the morning to squeeze me fresh orange juice. She walked me through her beautiful garden, a fragrant oasis in the depths of Detroit, and proudly showed me all the flowers she had planted. She prepared my favorite Hungarian dishes for dinner — chicken paprikash with homemade noodles, stuffed cabbage, and *székely gulyas*. When I was back home she sent me tins of Hungarian cookies cut in the shapes of hearts, moons, and stars, covered with powdered sugar. She spent every evening nestled on her couch doing needlework. She knitted me beautiful blankets and pieced together quilts with fabric from her old dresses. I continue to wrap myself in these blankets and can still feel her love around me.

Two decades after she died, I was at a crossroads in life. My memory of Nagymama and all that I had learned from her had faded considerably. I was in my fifth year of a PhD program at Harvard and felt strongly that I was not following my true path. I had given my mind plenty of opportunity to grow and develop, but I had neglected my heart and my hands, and these other parts of me were aching to express themselves. So at age thirty-six I left graduate school and decided to take my first art-making workshop at Turtle Studio, a community art studio in Watertown, Massachusetts.

Kate Ransohoff, the director, is a gifted artist and teacher with a unique ability to see people's potential and to help them create in their own voice. She encourages her students to grow their art and their lives in ways that are authentic, meaningful, and enriching. Kate led me to my spot of grace by gently helping me to get to the core of what I love and care deeply about in the world.

One day Kate did a guided visualization with some of us, taking us back through the years of our lives to discover the things that we had always loved, the things that lit us up and revealed the truth of who we really were. I was surprised to realize that my favorite things were the long-forgotten memories of my Hungarian family — the smells, tastes, sounds, and sights of my heritage. I remembered the treasure hunts I took through my grandparents' small home, with their plastic-covered couches and modest Americana furnishings. I uncovered beautiful handmade objects from Hungary that were in drawers and boxes in the attic. I discovered old dolls in traditional Hungarian costume, luscious laces, woven and embroidered textiles, colorful painted pottery, and animal-skin flasks.

Kate believes in the power of engaging creatively with materials with no particular goal or outcome in mind. She suggested that I bring in some of the things I had inherited from my Hungarian relatives and play with them. For the next five years I learned about Hungarian village culture and their "art of living," and I celebrated this in my own art-making. I discovered that what lights me up is not only making my own art but also witnessing all the ways that people around the world have used art and ceremony to mark the milestones of human life, from the cradle to the grave.

I have come to appreciate that every culture has its own spot of grace, its own unique ways of expressing the experience of what it is to be human.

I am forever grateful to my nagymama and to Kate for teaching me, in their different ways, to pay attention to what I love and to use my whole handcrafted self in service of sharing these passions with the world.

SINGING NAKED

ELISABETH GAINES • *Boston, Massachusetts*

My best friend, Chuck, loves my singing. He has told me innumerable times that he'd rather sing with me than do almost anything else in the world, aside from spending time with his kids. I don't hear my voice the way he does. I've sung for as far back as I can remember, mostly to myself, definitely along with records, and always in the school glee club or chorus. I haven't thought of singing as a gift; it's just what I do; it makes life brighter and sweeter.

Chuck and I met in the Mystic Chorale, a Boston-area community singing group. The first time he heard me sing a solo, he made a point of telling me how deeply he was moved by my voice, saying, "You sounded like you were singing *naked* up there!" Needless to say, that got my attention (although it didn't do anything to help my shyness about stepping into the spotlight).

One day, after we'd known each other a year or so, I picked up my guitar for the first time in years. Chuck walked into the room and stood there quietly, watching and listening. When I finished, he looked me straight in the eye and told me I should quit my job to become a folk singer. Now there's some faith for you! I haven't become a folk singer, but with his ceaseless support, I have begun to sing and lead songs on my own at gatherings of family and friends. I've been doing the singing, but Chuck made it happen. His absolute certainty that my singing brings value to the world has been pure grace to me.

fruit

At many times in my life I have been awakened to the responsibility I have to pass on the teachings of the wise and generally older guides in my life. No teachings are clearer than those I received from my friend Joan.

Joan and I were business associates. When we had lunch one day, Joan asked me about my family, and I soon found myself telling her about my four-year-old son, who was having seizures regularly. By the end of the conversation, Joan had drawn out of me the details of his condition and my thoughts regarding his treatment. With one question after another she encouraged me to share more than I had shared with almost anyone else. It was only later in our friendship that she told me the path she had been on as a mother some decades earlier with her son who, at a young age, had battled cancer.

After years of pondering her interest in me, I have come to realize that she was encouraging me to follow my deep passion to save my son's brain and to work harder to find a safe road for him — in essence, to salvage his future. She was the only person in my life who genuinely understood the isolation a mother feels when she has a severely sick child. Each doctor was able to take the condition only as far as his or her specialty. It took several years, various specialists, and a handful of wise experts to solve the puzzle of my son's brain.

Joan opened doors gently for me by sharing information,

spot of grace

> *It is up to you to illumine the earth.*
>
> PHILIPPE VENSIER

researching sources, and giving me the confidence to never stop seeking answers until I could hopefully find a cure. My son has been seizure free for three years now. When I come into contact with parents dealing with an ailing child, I pass on Joan's gift of compassion, curiosity, and caring. It is one way I can make a difference for others the way she did for me.

PAULA LAND • *Cedar Rapids, Iowa*

My classroom was filled with, shall we say, unique personalities and spirits. It seemed as though every challenging four- or five-year-old child was placed in my care. I looked at the other classes and thought how nice it would be to have such a "good" class of students. Little did I know at the time that my class would allow me to recognize my gift.

Roy was the first puzzle. He was a bundle of energy with few social skills. Trying to get Roy to do anything for more than sixty seconds was next to impossible. Circle time was a favorite of all the children — except Roy. He couldn't sit still, he disrupted the other children, and he wandered off. I tried many things to get him to conform and be attentive but to no avail. Finally, instead of resisting his energy, I started to observe it, live with it, and try to understand it. I began to figure out what made him tick. One day at circle time I set Roy at the back of the group and gave him a handful of LEGOs without saying anything. After we had settled in with our routine, I explained to the children that circle time was for listening and sharing together, which was difficult for Roy (this came as no surprise to them!) and that playing with LEGOs would help him be a good listener. At least I hoped so!

For once the group time was glorious. Mr. Bundle of Energy sat quietly in the back of the room, intently piecing together the various colors and shapes. At one point I asked the children a question. A little voice in back chimed in to provide the answer. It was Roy! He could finally participate in our shared experience. I could even see the delight in other children's eyes.

As the year went on, the children and I began to see difference as uniqueness, and we all began to appreciate the different way each person was special. One mother commented that her daughter, who hated to interact with adults, wouldn't stop talking about me. The little girl, who often felt anxious, knew that I could serve as solid ground for her when her anxiety bubbled to the surface.

At the end of the year I told the director that I thought she must not have liked me much because she placed all the challenging kids in my room. "No, Paula," she said. "I know that you have a talent for recognizing what children need and what special gifts they have to share with the world." I hadn't seen this in myself before. As a child, I had never thought I was special. I had wished that I had talent, like the girl who could paint or the boys who could play the piano or get straight As. It took a little boy who exasperated everyone else to help me see this special gift.

I don't teach anymore, and I miss the joy and wonder of watching children learn. However, I carry my gift into my work in the adult world. I am comfortable with my talent, and though people can't see it and I don't talk about it, I know that recognizing the value and gifts of others is my contribution to make.

fruit

WILL COCKRELL • *Carbondale, Colorado*

My mother handled the money for Tibet House when she worked on Wall Street. My father produced a series of television shows on Joseph Campbell, who was a famous mythologist. My parents raised me to explore all religions and let me choose what I liked or didn't like about each one.

About eight years ago, when I was eight, my mother was invited through her work for Tibet House to a gathering of about two hundred people at the Waldorf Hotel in New York. The Dalai Lama was going to present an award to the then wife of Harrison Ford, Melissa Mathison, for writing the screenplay *Kundun* (which means "Enlightened One" in Tibetan). I didn't really know who the Dalai Lama was. My mom dragged me to this event and made me wear a suit.

I had watched *Air Force One*, which stars Harrison Ford, about a dozen times during that month, and he was my hero. I mean, he hung outside of an airplane and played the president in the movie! While we were waiting for the Dalai Lama, my mom took me over to meet the real Harrison Ford, and I talked with him and got a picture taken of me with my awesome hero. I was in heaven.

Then we were all waiting in the room at the top of the Waldorf, and I stood next to my mom, surrounded by a few hundred people. They were all adults, and I was the youngest. The Dalai Lama entered the room and came directly over to me, took both my hands in his, and blessed only me out of all these people. Later, everyone told me how lucky I was and that this had been an omen. When we got home, my mom made me call my dad to tell him who I had met that night, and I told him, "Harrison Ford!" We laugh about that now.

I am now going into the tenth grade, and the spot of grace that the Dalai Lama found in me has made me want to go to Columbia University to study comparative religions. I have decided that I want to teach tolerance through understanding different religions, even though I know it won't pay much.

THE LAYUP SHOT

FRANCES L. WONG • *Brooklyn, New York*

It was a year after my father died. I was twelve. I was feeling terribly lonely and invisible, missing my dad. One day in a park, a Chinese man who wore glasses, a blue shirt, white pants, and a white tie limped up to me. He asked whether I would like to play basketball with the girls' team that he coached. I accepted hesitantly.

Days later I went to the gym with a friend. It was inside a church on Madison Street in Chinatown. I learned how to do a layup shot. The coach said that I knew exactly how to use my skills to score a basket. In three months I became the star shooter, making hook shots and jump shots. My nickname became Jabbar, after Kareem Abdul-Jabbar. I wore the number 33, the same number as Larry Bird, one of the best basketball players of all time. I became more confident and began to trust my instincts, and eventually I got to play with people from Japan, China, Hong Kong, and Taiwan. Through basketball, I came to understand the Chinese language and culture on a much deeper level. I was no longer just an invisible American-born Chinese girl. I had roots, and I had reach.

> *I don't know Who — or What — put the question, I don't know when it was put. I don't even remember answering. But at some moment I did answer Yes to Someone — or Something — and from that hour I was certain that existence is meaningful and that, therefore, my life, in self-surrender, had a goal.*
>
> DAG HAMMARSKJÖLD

I now work for a hospital in New York City, providing health care services and bridging the gap to the Chinese community. I'm fluent in four Chinese dialects. I've helped to develop a Chinese inpatient unit that is equipped with Chinese satellite TV stations, bilingual nurses and aides, and a Chinese menu. I have been able to get bilingual Chinese volunteers to come in and visit the patients daily so they can access more resources. Now that I think about it, that's exactly what the coach helped me to do: access more resources, both inside and outside myself. What the coach gave me that day in the park, I've been able to give back to my whole community. Who would have thought a layup shot would help me make such a difference!

fruit

KAREN KOSHGARIAN • *Mountain View, California*

I remember her sitting, smiling, in the front row as I struggled with the correct pronunciation of her name. This was high school, and as an art teacher, I wanted to make every student feel seen and welcomed. Even on the first day, she made eye contact with me and laughed at my jokes. That was so different from the usual distant teenage response that I immediately took notice of her.

She returned to my art classroom for three years, taking every subject I offered, eventually working up to the coveted position of art teacher's aid. I trusted her to unpack and label art supplies each September. She even had her own key to the cabinet where all the supplies were stored. Her work was impeccable, reliably the best she could do.

About a month before graduation, she became extremely depressed and unreachable. She stopped bantering with me, even though she came by to work every day. I had no idea what was going on, and I wanted to respect her privacy, so I didn't inquire about her sudden change of mood. I did, however, in the silence of those last few weeks, allow her to spend all her free time with me. I held the space as a sacred trust and allowed her to be as she wished.

We maintained a casual connection over the ensuing years. One day I was able to ask about those last weeks of high school. She told me that back then she didn't want to leave my classroom, which had been a safe harbor and place of inspiration for her. She was very

spot of grace

depressed about the possibility of never seeing me and never again having the luxury of the art room available to her.

In that moment I recognized how essential it is to hold the space of sacred trust for someone. In that space any one of us, like this student, can come to trust the best that is inside.

fruit

GIVING BACK

DONNA MUMMERY • *Wanganui, New Zealand*

I have spent almost every day of the past year and a half with my dad, who has been diagnosed with a memory disorder. My dad has always been loyal to his children; he has always encouraged me and would not let me say negative things about myself. During this year and a half, I could be loyal to him, making a difference as I did simple things, like making his lunch or checking on his room to see that he had everything he needed.

We shared a common past and acquaintances from a small town that he lived in for eighty years of his life. When he moved to a larger city to be closer to his now-grown children, we enjoyed talking about that common past together, and I think it helped him orient to a new beginning this late in life. I helped him remember his grandchildren's birthdays and make phone calls to his other beloveds. It was like being in the very heart of the family. This year and a half has brought the realization that in my father's eyes, I am a valid and successful individual, something all of us want and need to know. I have felt fulfilled, knowing I could bring value to a parent who has done so much for me over the years.

THE GIFT OF PASSION

ANNIE POWELL • *Belmont, Massachusetts*

I was a fifth-grade teacher in my early thirties, and I loved my work more than anything. I was fascinated by everything about "my kids," especially who they were and what made them tick. In an after-school workshop, I was first introduced to the idea of learning styles by a woman named Dr. Carolyn Tennant. I was so enthralled by what I was learning that I pursued her next course, a ten-week session offered in the mountains outside of town during the middle of winter.

> *We drop like pebbles into the ponds of each other's souls, and the orbit of our ripples continues to expand, intersecting with countless others.*
>
> JOAN BORYSENKO

She suggested we share the ride every week so that we wouldn't have to make what could be a treacherous drive alone.

One really snowy day, conditions were horrible and we nearly slid off the road. Even though we knew we would be late, for safety's sake we stopped at a little café for a cup of tea. We were engaged in a lively conversation about the experiences I'd been having with my students when she stopped me midsentence and said, "You know you're gifted, don't you?" Time stopped, and inside my head I became so silent I could hear the snow falling outside. The conversation continued, and we made it safely to class that day.

My fascination with human differences continues to grow, almost thirty years later. But Carolyn's gift to me goes beyond the specifics

fruit

209

of what I learned from her. I remember how I felt in that moment as clearly as I remember her words and the silence. It was as if she had said, "There you are!" I felt seen and appreciated in the core of my life, my unguarded passion apparent to someone else. As she acknowledged it, I embraced it, and since then I have never been the same.

STANDING UP FOR MOM

LI LU-PORTER • *Bellevue, Washington*

When I was growing up in China, my mom taught high-school English. She was known for her patience, love of learning, and sharing her knowledge. I remember waking up at night and seeing her still awake grading papers and adding just a few more comments for her students. She loved to hear stories about my days and experiences. We would take long walks after dinner and talk as if I were a grown-up. More than anything else, she encouraged me to have my voice.

One day during second grade, I came home from school quite upset about an event that had happened in the physical education class. The teacher had made some inappropriate requests of the students. I didn't think they were fair and talked to the teacher about it, but he didn't want to hear it and tried to silence me. After listening to my story and asking several clarifying questions, my mom took me to school and helped me dialogue with the teacher.

In this one act, my mother taught me to trust my instincts and value the place inside that they come from instead of blindly following the dictates of an authority. She supported me in having the courage to speak my truth, even if it was a nine-year-old's truth.

My mom has survived two battles with breast cancer and is now fighting another round. Since she loves uplifting stories, I want her to read this now and know that she taught me to find my voice at a young age and to trust that I matter. I hope it supports her the way she has always supported me.

fruit

FLYING FOR NONNA

SIMONE AMBER • *Brooklyn Heights, New York*

My grandmother Nonna lived in a Beirut apartment on the ground floor across the street from us. In her bedroom was an armchair facing the window so she could see what was happening outside. What I remember most is her patience with me. I recall none of her exact words, but to this day I remember how she made me feel when I walked into her home. She scooped me up and carried me into a special little room where she kept the great cookies she made. Some cookies were stuffed with pistachios, some with walnuts, some with dates.

It wasn't the cookies that made me feel so full. It was the quality of her presence; I could simply rest in it. I could just be, without any pressure or expectations to do anything. Now I realize that she had probably dreamed she'd have a granddaughter someday. I am her dream. She sat in that armchair, looking out that window, because she had nowhere else to go and no other opportunities to share herself with the world. I have a career and travel around the world doing what I can to make a difference. I am the bird flying for her.

spot of grace

GREAT-AUNT CATHERINE RAINBOW

PEGGY TILESTON • *Martha's Vineyard, Massachusetts*

I met my great-aunt Catherine only once in my life. She came to visit when I was in second grade. She was so tall! When she heard that I was learning piano, she sat pressed up against me on the bench and taught me to play "Melancholy Baby." There were no notes to look at and no piano teacher to tell me I was playing it wrong. There was just Great-Aunt Catherine, patient and attentive, laughing and warm, seeing *me*.

Her parting gift to me was a crystal heart pendant on a string that shone rainbows in the sun. Soon after that we moved to a different town — another continent, actually — and I was the new girl. Everything was so different in third grade. Memories of much of that year are gone, but I remember sitting in my closet clutching that pendant in my hand for dear life. That was the year I was sexually molested by a neighbor, which didn't surface in my mind until much later. The story I tell myself now and feel in my heart is that Great-Aunt Catherine's music and talisman and her seeing me were like a gentle caress on my brow. Her blessing was hearing my music, seeing my heart. It had such a powerful effect on me that I've done what I can to pass it on. I have chosen work as a residential youth counselor that gives me the good fortune to acknowledge a young person's spot of grace on a daily basis.

Today I said good-bye to Ruben, who had been at the hospital for ten days because he suffered such debilitating anxiety attacks that he

fruit

had not left his room at home for three months. Ruben looks like someone you don't want to mess with. He grew up in the projects, became a heroin addict, packed a gun and dealt drugs, and was respected and feared by his peers, a leader on the streets. He decided to quit heroin cold turkey alone in his room and for that he earned even more respect on the street. He continued to deal drugs while staying clean because he is the main breadwinner for his family and he has a daughter. Besides, it's hard to give up the bling when you've had it. He got caught, did jail time, had his first anxiety attack, went home, and started dealing again.

The attacks kept coming, he got busted again, and he ended up in the hospital. From here he'll be going back to jail. While he is here, he is a leader: warm, friendly, caring, encouraging to his peers. He says he wants to turn his life around so it'll mean something more than bling.

I've been teaching him about breathing, about putting a space between impulse and action, about grounding and centering and even meditation. He is soaking up the learning. Today in his last group he practiced finding his center no matter how he was provoked. The group applauded, and I told them that whenever they think of Ruben to think about him grounded, centered, solid, and calm and to send him that energy. I told him I believe he is a leader and a teacher and suggested that since he's going to be practicing this stuff daily, he teach his cell mates how to center and ground and meditate. "Can you see it?" I asked him. He smiled a yes. What a blessing!

Jazzia was wiry, tough, closed, and grim when she walked into the office for the intake interview. She wouldn't speak. Her foster mother said she was getting into fights at school, was disobeying the rules, and was defiant, angry, and uncontrollable. Jazzia stared at the floor while she spoke. Time was almost up. I suggested her mom leave, then I asked Jazzia what she loved most in the world. She looked up, startled, and then replied, "My baby brothers."

"What else?"

She looked away shyly and said softly, "Singing."

"I love it too." I said. "See you next week."

The next week I took her out of the tiny office and down to the basement rec room. I sang her a welcome song in which I invited her to sing me how her week went. She looked delighted and then scared and shy, so I sang, "Repeat after me," and sang, "My week really sucked." She laughed and sang back to me. By the end of the session, she was singing her heart out in that big empty room. She didn't show up the next week, and when I called her foster mother, she said, "Oh, she was sent into residential treatment." I never saw her again. Great-Aunt Catherine and I send you this blessing, Jazzia: may your music carry you over all the rough spots in your life and pull you into joy.

ONE TENNIS BALL, ONE FAMILY

RONNIE R. LOHR • *Houston, Texas*

I love baseball, and one of the true joys in my life is coaching young kids, encouraging them to have fun and success. I will never forget one ten-year-old boy in particular. Rodney was an awkward child with little athletic ability. His parents came to every practice and every game, but Rodney knew that he was an embarrassment to his dad because he could not do anything as well as anyone else.

I could see that he had trouble with his eye-hand coordination, so we practiced several drills of watching the ball come into the glove. Rodney slowly began to catch on, but he still took the field with his head down as if he were dreading that a ball might be hit to him.

At a critical moment in a game, with runners on all bases, a high fly ball was hit directly at Rodney. His parents cringed, but he remembered his lessons and watched the ball come right into his glove. In this one act he prevented the runs from scoring and allowed his team to win the game. His parents cheered so hard and so loud, and Rodney came off of the field with his head held high. He had done it!

> *We are here to add to the sum of human goodness. To prove the thing exists. And however futile each individual act of courage or generosity, self-sacrifice or grace, it still proves the thing exists. Each act adds to the fund.*
>
> JOSEPHINE HART

At that moment Rodney realized how much his parents cared for him. It was much more than catching a ball. It was a family that found each other. Rodney had never missed a game, nor had his parents, but from that game on, that family came together to the ball games.

All it took was thirty minutes of exercises to help Rodney's co-ordination and build his confidence over his fear of a hard ball. This short time with him made me realize that we all have it in us to share ourselves in small ways that can change someone else's life forever.

fruit

I was twelve years old when I figured out that my calling in life was to become a mother. Somehow years passed, and I earned multiple degrees and climbed the corporate ladder. Despite all this, I never could let go of my longing to become a mother, though I never married. Without much emotional support from my family, I decided to submit my dossier to China to adopt a baby girl. When the day came on which I received a postage stamp–sized photo of my daughter, I called my parents with the excitement of walking in a dream. I was a mother! I was crushed when they offered only disapproval.

Shortly after 9/11 I got on the plane and met my daughter in Wuhan, China. Right then and there I knew it was the best life decision I had ever made. Emilia clung to me and for weeks would not go to anyone else. My parents came to visit. Emilia was sitting on the floor. My father took one look at her, opened his arms up, and said, "Ella," which means "come here" in Greek. Emilia raised her arms, and they embraced. In that moment my father and I forgave each other, and it has been a love fest ever since. This little Chinese girl gave my Greek father his greatest name: Papou, "grandfather."

When it was time for Emilia to start kindergarten, we attended meet-the-teacher night as a family — Claire, my second daughter adopted from China, Emilia, and me. As we entered the school Claire piped up, "Sissy, is there a playground here?" Emilia quickly gave her an annoyed, older-sister look and said, "Claire, I am here to study, not to play!" When her teacher bent down and asked her what she wanted to learn in kindergarten, Emilia replied, "Mrs. Hornbeck, I want to be a doctor, so if you could, please help me with that!"

The next day, I complied with Emilia's request to have her hair curled. (Have you ever tried to curl Asian hair?) As we headed for the door, I paused and asked if she wanted to take a little part of China to school with her. "Of course," she said. "The bracelet." So I found the red-thread-and-jade beaded bracelet that I bought when I went to China to get Emilia. I found myself in tears, thinking about the woman who gave birth to her and the mystery of her first year in China.

When it was time to drop her off, I gave her my infamous lipstick kiss on her hand and whispered my favorite parting line: "Remember who you are." Without missing a beat, Emilia responded, "The Linos girl!"

Both of my daughters help me remember, on a daily basis, that I make a difference and that as a mother I am living and giving from a blessed place.

fruit

KONG

BARBARA BROWNING • *Arcata, California*

Lane was a lost and undefined teenager who found my spot of grace. He was a severely mentally retarded young adult I worked with at my first job in a residential care facility. He was labeled as one of the most difficult kids, and I suppose he was for most of the staff, but he and I shared some kind of affinity, and when he was with me his behavior problems disappeared. My schedule of working with him was erratic, but he seemed to know when I would be coming back, and he was always waiting outside the building each time I arrived.

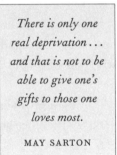

There is only one real deprivation . . . and that is not to be able to give one's gifts to those one loves most.

MAY SARTON

After many months I had to leave the job, and I didn't go back to the facility for several years. When I finally returned, there was Lane. He looked into my eyes for several seconds, then lifted his hand and put it up to my forehead and said, "Kong," our secret greeting.

For much of my life, until I met Lane, I had felt invisible, but he saw a light from within me and connected to it. I have never since felt as if I don't matter.

spot of grace

About ten years ago, I was on a plane going west, and a young woman boarded and sat across the aisle from me. I noticed her for two reasons. She was very attractive, and she was holding a teddy bear about half her size. After she sat down, I teased her by asking if she had a ticket for the bear. She laughed and said no, and we settled into the hermetically sealed bubbles that airline passengers adopt to create privacy around themselves.

About halfway through the flight she popped the bubble by leaning over and saying, "I just told that man sitting by the window a lie. He asked me why I was going to Tucson, and I told him to visit relatives, but I am really going to enter rehab." She proceeded to share her life story with me, which included family issues, abuse, and drug use. She had been working as an exotic dancer, which meant that she took her clothes off for money. That lifestyle had led her down a dark path to drugs, alcohol, and offers of prostitution and pornography. As I listened to her story, I marveled at all she had gone through, and I came to realize that though she was the age of my daughters, she had already lived more in her twenty years than I would ever live.

In spite of all of this, there was a sweet resilience to her, a clarity about what had gone wrong in her life, and a determination to turn it around. I listened to all she shared and told her I was sure she was going to make it, based on her story and demeanor. At the end of the

fruit

221

flight, she thanked me for listening to her and told me I had saved her life. I smiled at her exuberance and wished her well.

A few years later, I got a note in the mail saying, "Wow, it's been five years since we met on that plane taking me to rehab. I thought you might like to know how I am doing. It is amazing how you touched my life. I will never forget you." She went on to tell me that she had managed to stay away from drugs, had been working for a radio station, and had recently gotten engaged. She felt she had achieved things she could not have imagined that day on the plane. It turned out that I was going to be traveling to the city to which she had moved, and we agreed to set up a time to get together.

When I saw her, she was still the attractive young woman I remembered, but this time she was dressed elegantly, with a poise and confidence found in few twenty-five-year-olds. She hugged me and told me I was her guardian angel and that little conversation we had had turned her life around. She had boarded the plane doubting anything would work in her life, and my affirmation of her as a person and of her possibilities had given her the last bit of strength she needed to work through her problems.

While that exchange had proved to be a spot of grace for her, I think it was an even greater one for me. I am quite sure that I said nothing profound or meaningful on that flight. What made all the difference was taking the time to connect to her, one spirit to another. It reminded me that we are all here to act as angels to each other. What a wonderful job we have been given! And what wonderful gifts we receive in doing that work!

A LESSON FOR THE TEACHER

LARRY L. DLUGOSH • *Lincoln, Nebraska*

When I began my public school science teaching career, Jerry was a sophomore in my biology class. He was a likable guy, but he slept quite a bit during the class. One day, while we were having a stirring discussion about the importance of nutrition, I woke Jerry and asked him if he could tell the class about nutrition. I intended to embarrass him for sleeping on the job.

Jerry said, "Let me see — nutrition. This morning my old man came home drunk at four AM. He got us all out of bed and beat us up. He then made us do chores, and after chores I had a piece of lunchmeat wrapped around a pickle for breakfast. There — that is my story about nutrition."

While I had intended to make an example of Jerry, he taught me the greatest lesson a teacher can learn: know where your students come from, and be a blessing to them, not a curse. I apologized for my behavior and let him know that if he needed any help I would be available. From time to time, Jerry came to me with questions about life after high school, the military, sports, and so on. I moved to a new school in a different community and then received a visit that first September from Jerry, home on leave from the air force.

Years later, at the thirty-fifth reunion of Jerry's graduating class, I saw him for the first time in more than three decades. I was a university professor working with teachers who wanted to become principals. I told Jerry that I spoke about him to every class I taught. I

fruit

223

explained that I thought I could help teachers be more student focused through "our" story. He looked surprised and responded that he talked to his family about me very often. I too was puzzled and recounted the incident in sophomore biology class. Jerry said, "I don't remember that incident. All I remember is that you cared about me as a person and helped me through a tough time in my life. That is what I tell my kids about."

To this day, I believe I live in a state of grace. Maybe it is because Jerry taught me how to be kind instead of controlling, caring instead of critical. It was fortunate Jerry was asleep in biology: otherwise, the chance to become mature may not have come so quickly for me.

ACOUSTIC MASSAGE

HERON SALINE • *San Francisco, California*

When I was growing up, my parents wanted each of the kids in our family to study a musical instrument. There was something powerful for me in hearing clear, steady, lively beats and rolls come out of a person's hands, so I chose drum lessons. I soon got bored with looking at little *x*'s and dots on the sheet music and trying to play someone else's rhythms. In second grade I gave up the drums and switched to piano, but I ran into the same challenge with reading sheet music: when I looked at the page, my hands just no longer knew where they were or what to do! I started memorizing the pieces note by note and staring at the sheet music during my lessons, pretending to read it while my hands played the song so I wouldn't get into trouble. When they figured this out, my teacher and parents agreed that since I was teaching myself, I could drop the lessons. I was in heaven. Over the years I became skilled enough to play ragtime in the dark!

> *Thank God our time is now when wrong comes up to meet us everywhere, never to leave us till we take the longest stride a soul folk ever took.*
>
> CHRISTOPHER FRY

When I was in my twenties, I used to hike to a hippie beach near Minneapolis where people gathered near the lake with conga drums, wood blocks, and other rhythm instruments. Their sounds were like some wild, magical part of that place. I felt shy listening to them and yet hungry to join in with the dance of booms and bops. Finally one

fruit

225

day I went over and sat on a log just to be near them. Deep in my mind, I heard myself say, "I can do this."

Fifteen years later, I play percussion instruments at many events, teach people how to notice and work with their inner rhythms, and have synthesized my own sound healing technique called acoustic massage. Now I realize I never would have been able to make the difference I do if I had been able to read music. It was in me all the time!

KEEPING MATT ALIVE

ANNE MCGINLEY • *Cortez, Colorado*

School is very difficult for my students, who are Navajo. Most of them are with me because they have had bad experiences in other school settings. Only a few consider themselves talented. Matt was no exception.

Matt carried a rage so deep that some days I knew just to stay out of his face. He and I got to know each other on a different plane of learning. If you could tiptoe around the rage, he was very smart and an incredible artist. Eventually the rage got him in trouble, and Matt was expelled.

The day after he left, the office assistant delivered a tube with a rope around it. It was the most incredible drawing, of children with empty eyes and huge frowns on their faces. I didn't know where it had come from, so I asked my students. They knew it came from Matt. Seeing the world through his eyes made me cry. His capacity to recognize and represent the pain around him changed forever the way I see. I keep him alive in me by telling his story to you.

NAVIGATING BY HEART

KAREN BALDWIN • *Omaha, Nebraska*

Growing up in western Kansas in the 1920s and '30s, with a band of wild brothers, my mother was never cognizant of gender. If she wanted to do something, she did it. When her oldest brother decided to learn to fly, she soon followed suit. Maybe it's no coincidence that my mother started to fly in 1937, the same year that Amelia Earhart, from Atchison, Kansas, took her famous round-the-world flight.

Mom's love of aviation took her into another uncharted territory for women, air traffic control. During World War II she worked in the Kansas City and Omaha air traffic control towers. She often told the story of a pilot from Oklahoma not wanting to take landing directions from a woman. She told him, "Fine, you can just circle all night because there's only two of us here for the next twelve hours, and we're both female!"

While I have many stories of my mother leading the way for women's rights, she never claimed to be a feminist. She just did what she wanted when the passion took hold of her. She found ways around all of the gender roadblocks.

Growing up with a courageous, bold woman to guide me influenced me in ways I never realized until much later in life. I too took a career path not shared by many women, banking — not because I wanted to make a statement but because it's the path I chose to follow as my unique way of making a difference in the world. As my mother always told us, "Follow your heart, and you'll always enjoy the life you created!"

spot of grace

RONITA JOHNSON • *Pleasant Hill, California*

I was sitting in class in my ninth-grade year when I received a note from my teacher to come to the counselor's office. Perplexed about what I might have done wrong, I slipped out quietly and walked bewildered to her office. Mrs. Kennedy was a stout woman with large, black-rimmed glasses, and our previous conversations had always been serious ones about my education. As I entered her office, she waved her hand, beckoning me to come in and sit down. Nervously I obeyed.

She came around and sat next to me. "I've noticed that you bite your fingernails," she said. It was true. I was a nervous child and would take it out on my nails. She continued, "You are a beautiful and special child, and you have wonderful hands." She pulled out a little leather pouch with tiny utensils while telling me, "You will touch many people with these hands." She took one hand and then the other, gently pushing back my cuticles and trimming the jagged edges of each finger. As she tended my fingers, she spoke to me like a fairy godmother about who I would become. She finished by smoothing sweet-smelling lotion on each hand.

I left there floating, head held high, with the biggest smile on my face, as if I really mattered. I never bit my nails again. I never forgot about Mrs. Kennedy. And I have touched many lives with these hands, through my music and life journeys.

A woman joined our church. She didn't know how to express

fruit

229

herself, and she often put herself down. During a class for new members, she confided in me that she was a drug addict and sold her body to get fixes. She had tried to quit dozens of times, but each time she found herself using and back on the street. I hugged her and said, "Your life matters. You have a gift to contribute that only you can give." She kept coming to church. Each time, I hugged her and reminded her that her life mattered. Sometimes I wouldn't see her for a couple of weeks, and when she returned, she'd tell me she had "fallen off" again. I kept putting my arms around her and telling her, "Your life matters." It took four years, but she is now clean, sober, and off the street. Helping other addicts and prostitutes has become her ministry. She has told me that during times of temptation, the words I learned from Mrs. Kennedy, "Your life matters," have helped her to remember who she really is.

MCDONALD'S ANGEL

LAWSON DRINKARD • *Big Timber, Montana*

Several summers ago a client asked me to travel to the East Coast to facilitate a "partnering" meeting at a public university. The meeting included architects, engineers, contractors, faculty, and university planners. I had been warned in advance that the meeting was likely to be contentious, as there was a history of unsuccessful projects between some of the participants.

I traveled to the university late the night before during a furious thunderstorm and struggled during the downpour to find parking and the guest accommodations provided for me. The room turned out to be a bare cinderblock room in a vacant first-year dormitory with a plastic-covered mattress and one fluorescent light in the ceiling. There was no phone, no Internet connection, and no bedside lamp. My plans for completing preparations for the meeting were nixed, so I went to bed with the idea of getting up early the next morning to complete my work.

I rose with the sun and ventured out of the university boundaries, where the only restaurant I could find open was a McDonald's. I carried my notes and files into the restaurant hoping to get a large cup of coffee and do my work. My inner voice was chattering rapidly, telling me over and over again that nothing had gone right on this trip so far, that I probably wouldn't be well prepared for the meeting, and that it was unlikely I'd do a very good job.

I ordered a large cup of coffee and proceeded to the condiments

fruit

counter to doctor it with sugar and cream. The area was small, and I had to wait a few moments behind a tall, scruffy-looking man. When he turned to face me, I said, "Good morning."

"How are you?" he asked.

"Terrific," I said — my standard answer to that question, though I didn't really mean it in this case.

After a long pause, he said, "It's good to be alive, isn't it? Somebody didn't make it yesterday, and we've been blessed with another opportunity."

I knew in an instant that I had been touched by an angel in the center of my chest and had experienced a powerful moment of grace. My attitude shifted, and I proceeded to the meeting with joy in my heart. During the course of the meeting I told this story, and it seemed to wake everybody else up the way it had me. I think from now on when people ask me, "How are you?" I'm going to reply, "Glad to be alive," and remember to mean it.

> *I'm becoming more and more myself with time. I guess that's what grace is. The refinement of your soul through time.*
>
> JEWEL

THE RIGHT STUFF

DAN LEFFEL • *McKinney, Texas*

Our two sons were home from college for the weekend. My wife had baked cookies for the occasion and lovingly put about a dozen into two plastic bags, one for each son to take back to school. Our older son, however, had eaten most of his before he left and was lamenting the fact that he hadn't saved enough cookies for the trip back. Our younger son had not yet eaten any of his, so I jokingly suggested he just open his brother's bag and take a few for the ride. "Your brother will never know," I said. Our older son turned to me, looked straight into my eyes, and said seriously, "Yes, but I would know." I was inspired, awestruck, and then proud of this demonstration of character from our son. My wife and I had made a difference! Somehow, during all of the challenges and tribulations of raising children in today's world, something had gone very right.

ALIVE IN HER MIND

TORAH CHRISTINA BEIJBOM • *Lund, Sweden*

What happened to me today is a seemingly small thing. I spoke with my dear friend Ingeborg, who is ninety-one, living alone after her husband passed away many years ago. I said I just wanted to hear how she was getting on. She said, "Oh, good that you called. I really just need to talk to someone."

For many days I hadn't talked to anyone; I had called Ingeborg because I too needed to talk. To hear my own voice when I have been silent for a long time is a door out to the world. "Talking to you helps me remember that I exist," I told her. She was delighted. We were both happy to share in this simple way.

Then she reminded me about a time when I drove her home after a lunch date. We stopped at the cemetery where my father is buried. I needed to put some flowers there.

"It was so beautiful," she said. "Sometimes cemeteries are so dead, but this one was alive and silent at the same time. The trees were magnificent. I can see it so clearly in front of me, the way you changed the flowers. This picture brings me joy and happiness."

A rush of energy went through my whole body. I felt so grateful to be in her picture — that when she sees this picture in her mind, it makes her happy and I am in it! A seemingly small thing. It makes me feel that I matter.

THE VOICE OF AN ANGEL

BETH COCKRELL • *Carbondale, Colorado*

From the outside, you wouldn't have known it was the worst of times. I was a successful stockbroker on Wall Street. I had incredible clients — artistic, famous, interesting people — and I worked with a number of charities in New York. I had found my niche and protected people from being taken by financial charlatans. Underneath it all, however, I felt worthless. My first marriage was short-lived.

Ten years later I married a doctor and had the "perfect life." After our son was born, my then husband began to beat me, which fed directly into my low self-esteem. During this time I received a notice from the IRS that I owed over $700,000 in back taxes simply because I had filed a joint tax return with my first husband. He had invested in tax shelters before I met him. He prepared the tax returns, was taking the deductions from the tax shelters he had invested in, and I, in blind faith, just signed the tax returns. I went to tax court expecting victory. Incredibly, I lost my case.

One day, after the last beating I received from my second husband, I fled with my son, never to see my home or belongings again. I later discovered that my second husband had a long history of abusing women. Shortly thereafter, I was invited to a party, dragged my depressed self there, and began a conversation with a man who was a journalist. I told him of my plight with the IRS and how they were going to take everything I had made on my own after my first marriage. He

fruit

wrote an article about my situation that was published in a very well-known magazine.

Galvanized and optimistic, I called a reporter at the *Wall Street Journal*, who published my story on the front page of that paper, including my address, a post office box I had rented. A few days later I went to the post office. The box was jammed so full that I had to retrieve the rest of the mail from the counter. I had hundreds of letters from other women who poured out their stories to me, women who were raising children with no child support, who also had the IRS garnishing their pay due to the misdeeds of their deadbeat ex-husbands.

I collapsed on my bed, sobbing, as I read these horror stories. I answered each one because these women were looking to me for hope. I decided that if I was going to lose everything, I would go down with guns blazing. The only problem was that I was terrified of having to speak in public. The voices in those letters, however, overpowered my fear.

I appealed to the Second Circuit Court of Appeals, where the hearing was attended by and reported on by many famous journalists. I lost in the appellate court, but some senators in Washington became interested because it was an election year. I was asked to testify before the Senate Finance Committee. I so wanted to testify, but I was sure I would have a panic attack and not be able to say a word if I were to speak live in front of Newt Gingrich or Trent Lott, to say nothing of all those cameras. In the interim, I took my case all the way to the Supreme Court, but they refused to hear it. I was on the hook for $700,000 — more money than I could ever repay.

The press on my case was hot. I shared some of the letters I was still receiving from other women who were in the same position. I couldn't allow my fear to win over the opportunity to tell these heartfelt stories. I decided to be their voice. I did testify before Congress. Me, the nobody who was terrified to speak in public. I found my voice and used it for all these silent women. I stood up proud and strong, live on national television, in front of every lawmaker and reporter, with a confidence I had never known before. I was telling those women's stories. I was telling my own.

> *Life is occupied in both perpetuating itself and in surpassing itself; if all it does is maintain itself, then living is only not dying.*
>
> SIMONE DE BEAUVOIR

Even though I lost in all the courts, the *Wall Street Journal* said I won in the court of public opinion. The stories in the press and appearances on many television shows paid off because Congress decided to change the law regarding joint tax returns. I went to the White House for the signing of the new *IRS Restructuring and Reform Act of 1998*. I spoke personally with President Clinton. Thousands more letters and cards came from women who wanted to thank me. They called me their angel, but they were my angels because they helped me find my self-worth, my self-respect, and, most important, my voice.

THE SMALLEST OF THINGS

THE REV. MARJEAN BAILEY • *Kennebunkport, Maine*

Sometimes all it takes is a tiny gesture to help you remember who you really are at your core and to help you live from that place for the rest of your life. When I was a little girl, we sat in the back row of church because my mother was afraid that I would make some kind of disturbance. She was very strict, and the people who sat in the back row with us knew it. Mr. James, a tall, dignified banker who wore brown tweed suits and put his hat under the pew, sat back there too. One Sunday he brought me a peach pit with a monkey carved into it. The carving was shiny and polished. He whispered in my ear, "I made this for you because you have such a good heart." I was amazed he saw that and have never forgotten that one person saw what was precious in me. I'm over seventy now, and to this day I can remember his words and tone of voice.

Decades later, I was walking down the street in Ann Arbor, Michigan, when two or three tough young men, real ruffians, came toward me. They seemed quite hostile, and I was a little frightened. I held back, wondering what was going to happen. When I got closer, I smiled to them from the goodness in my heart, and we walked past each other. They called to me, "Hey, who are you?" All of the hostility had disappeared. As they walked away, one of them said, "Hey, that lady's real cool." Isn't it amazing how one small grace-filled moment of recognition can grow and reach so many other people across time and space?

spot of grace

orchard

If You Knew That the World Needed What Only You Could Bring, How Would You Live?

We can all be angels to one another. We can choose to obey
the still small stirring within, the little whisper that says, "Go. Ask.
Reach out. Be an answer to someone's plea. You have a part to play. . . ."
The world will be a better place for it.
And wherever they are, the angels will dance.

JOAN WESTER ANDERSON, *Where Angels Walk*

My mother taught me how to add. She was always adding up how much we had and how much other people had and how much everything cost. My sister taught me to subtract. She was always subtracting how much attention I got from how much attention she got. My father taught me to divide. He divided the world into two sides: the good guys and the bad guys, the right guys and the wrong guys, the ones who would make it and the ones who wouldn't.

It was my grandmother who taught me to multiply. Making a loaf of Sabbath bread on Friday morning was her favorite teaching tool. As she kneaded the dough, she said, "This is what the world does to you sometimes. It stretches you, and pushes you around, and turns you over, and slaps you into shape. This is so the gifts you brought into the world get stronger, *ketzaleh.*"

Then her long, crafty fingers patted the dough round and sprinkled flour all over, as if it were a baby's tush. After cradling it into a large glass bowl, she let me blanket it with an immaculate towel and place it gently near the stove.

"Now comes the magic. We'll go clean the house for Shabbat. By the time we are finished, the magic will have happened."

"What's the magic, Grandma? Tell me."

Her face crinkled like white taffeta as she smiled and said, "Just come back every fifteen minutes and peek. You'll see the magic."

And I did. While she washed and dusted and folded, I kept running into the kitchen, lifting the towel, and peeking at the golden, round baby bread. Nothing. But I didn't give up. I trusted Grandma completely.

Finally, when I lifted the towel I saw that the bread had grown into a golden balloon that filled the whole bowl. I ran to tell her about the magic.

I dragged her back to the kitchen to show her what had happened. Her eyes sparkled as she laughed. "*Ketzaleh*, it really isn't magic. It's the yeast that makes it rise twice as big." I must have looked crushed, because she placed a floury hand on my forehead and said, "But, my darling, watch what happens now. This is really something."

Then she turned the dough out of the bowl and plopped it onto the floury counter, stretching, slapping, stretching, slapping until the dough was a thick, flat disc.

"Grandma, you're killing it!" I squealed.

"No, my precious. This will help the bread rise even higher than before. It will make the dough stretchy and strong."

Once again she rubbed flour all over it and placed the bowl back near the stove. "Now, you keep peeking like you did before, and let me know when that dough is twice as big. Then I'll tell you about the *real* magic."

Faithfully, I kept peeking. Sure enough, the bread multiplied. As she squeezed the dough into three thick snakes, I asked her, "Grandma, do people have yeast inside them? Is that what makes us grow bigger?"

"In people, it's the life force that makes your body grow, but there's another kind of yeast that makes your soul grow."

Leaning toward me, she whispered the next words slowly, right into my ear. "We call it love. Love for the people in your family, and for your friends. Love for the people in your neighborhood, everywhere, and for all the animals and plants in the world."

In my grandmother's mystical tradition, it is taught that we are angels to one another. It is said that we are sent, without our knowledge, to various places in order to do our destined work and make love multiply. Thus any person on earth may be called upon to act as an unwitting angel for another. Once I became aware of this possibility, the opportunities seemed to multiply endlessly.

It's time to ignite a small revolution, a revolution of angels carrying stories to balance the darkness. How do you ignite a revolution? It's not really such a big deal, if you think about it. Revolution means a turning — turning around, turning over, turning toward. Turning as night turns into day or cold turns into warmth.

Revolutions begin gradually. Dawn emerges when the thick velvet sky fills slowly with light. Day emerges from night, wakefulness from sleep, and warmth from cold. There is another side to everything. This is the way life works.

I am wondering, what is the other side of trauma — the daylight balance to trauma's dark night? Painful events in childhood can mark one for life, freezing a person's capacity to yeast his or her own life and use it to nourish others. Can happy events mark us for life as well with a sense of buoyancy, permeability, and connection? If *trauma* is a moment of wounding, pain, and distress, what do we call the moments when we are healed, blessed, and blissed, moments when we recognize or ignite the light in ourselves, each other, and the world? If traumatic moments can create a disconnection from ourselves and from that which we love, then there must also be moments that mark us with an ongoing sense of resilience. I have searched in every dictionary and thesaurus I have for an antonym for the word and have found nothing.

I believe the other side of trauma is a moment of grace. How would children grow if they were continually reminded of their unique ways of contributing to the world? How would you be different if your mind sourced your epiphanies as often as it does your mistakes and failures? What if acknowledging another's spot of grace was as easy as commenting on their limitations? What if you developed a fluency in articulating other people's senseless gifts of beauty?

At a retreat we facilitated in Sundance, Utah, called Time Out, my son, David, and his wife, Angie, interviewed and videotaped each participant for fifteen minutes. They asked the participants to talk about a range of topics, including what they did for work, what they truly loved, and what mattered most to them. In almost every case, when we viewed the video later, each person's spot of grace was obvious to all of us; even the most skeptical in the group could see the person being interviewed light up and shine when speaking about what they loved, as if they held the moon in their mouths.

Remember Patrick Burke's story, "Following the Thread," about how his athletic ability was ignited because a veteran triathelete recognized it and invited him to participate on bike rides? (See page 76.) If you follow the thread of that story a little longer, it leads to another story that illustrates how little it takes to multiply this illumination.

Patrick's story arrived in my inbox at just the right moment. The previous night my son, David, had been telling me he felt bummed; it was one of those moments we all trudge through when everything feels hard. Several of his closest friends had been wildly successful, and he felt as if he just couldn't get it together. At forty, he thought he should be doing something more with his life, achieving more, making a difference somehow. David is a superb athlete who prefers single-person sports — skiing, surfing, golf, windsurfing. He was training for a two-hundred-mile, one-day bike race through the mountains of Utah and Wyoming, a goal far beyond anything he had ever achieved. At this point he didn't think he'd be able to finish.

Patrick had attended a Time Out retreat with him. The day Patrick's story arrived, I emailed back and asked if he minded if I sent it on to David because I thought it might help. This was Patrick's reply:

> I'm really moved that you asked. I can so relate. I know the familiar ache he's feeling better than I've ever fully articulated — the go-it-alone approach, the knife's edge of fear at having not achieved enough. It's very lonely, no matter how much those around try to help out.
>
> I wonder if David knows he's been one of those unmentioned people I wrote about. I remember when I first met

him at Time Out. Beyond all the history of shame and failure I recounted, Dave related to me only based on what I wanted to create in my life. He saw then what I couldn't see in myself. Without knowing it, he has secured such a place in my heart that if there is *any* way that I can be there for him, particularly on an issue so dead center in my own life, I would do so in a heartbeat. As a guy who outwardly looks to the world as if he has a million friends and inwardly thinks he has to do it all solo, I rather suck at reaching out. So just send this right on to him. Maybe the two of us can remind each other we don't have to go it alone.

Sometimes we follow patterns that are too small for us, that focus and develop only a small part of who we really are. Sometimes the forces around us trap us into noticing all that is not possible. The life in us may be squeezed, like bread dough, into a shape that is not really our own. What is it that enables certain people to respond differently to what might flatten the rest of us? Are only a few remarkable people able to sing while being incarcerated, create while everything around them is being destroyed, find wisdom in the midst of depravity? Or are such people bearers of the possible, living their lives like a flag that reminds the rest of us what lies within: the possibility of leaping across the habitual abysses carved in our minds to make different choices — choosing, in effect, to perceive, think, and act as fully free human beings?

The people who have been my greatest guides, those known and never met, are individuals who grew as a result of the crucible events that life brought them instead of being destroyed by them. They find opportunity where others find only despair. They choose to live inside questions that widen their periphery. They choose to influence their own and others' destinies in a positive way. They have tapped into a resource that is available to each of us.

Not just a special few are born with this capacity; it resides in each of us. I call it spiritual courage. It is choosing to grow the spot of grace in yourself and others on behalf of what is healthiest in the world. It is refusing to humiliate yourself or allow anyone else to suffer that diminishment. Ultimately, it is choosing to do with your life something that enhances freedom and elevates human dignity. Simply put, spiritual courage is the courage to care.

How Do You Turn Toward What Really Matters?

This is not a time to live without a practice. It is a time when all of us will need the most faithful, self-generated enthusiasm (enthusiasm: to be filled with god) in order to survive in human fashion.... We must ask what is my practice? What is steering this boat that is my fragile human life?... Whatever it is, now is the time to look for it, to locate it, definitely, and put it to use.

ALICE WALKER, *We Are the Ones We Have Been Waiting For*

Pick a day, any day. Make the commitment to yourself that you will listen and watch for what lights up the people you meet and that you will then acknowledge it.

For instance, during a long phone call with an associate at work

orchard

who has facilitated a particularly difficult conversation, just before you hang up, you might casually allude to how that person made a difference: "I was about ready to give up when I heard what the agenda was, Catherine, but you facilitated so effectively that we seemed to fly through it. I felt as if you were holding the kite string just taut enough that we didn't get lost, while letting the conversation soar when it needed to. You seem to have a special capacity for creating order out of chaos."

Or, as you are walking the building super to the door of your apartment after he has unclogged your drains at two in the morning, you might pause with your hand on the knob and say, "I have noticed, Paul, that you are consistently here for me when I most need it. It really means a great deal to know that in an emergency, you keep your cool and take charge."

Notice the effect this has on your energy, your sense of belonging and connection. Like practicing random acts of kindness, acknowledging someone else's spot of grace, no matter how he or she responds, ignites your own. You simply feel fuller.

Last year I asked a group of about a thousand people to do this between sessions at a three-day conference. Instead of having a brief chat with someone in the elevator or lobby and then walking away, I suggested that they listen to the other person, search for the spot of grace, and acknowledge verbally the moments they saw him or her light up. "When you spoke about systems dynamics, Linda, your eyes started sparkling and your words got very alive. It was exciting to listen to you." I'm sure some of the people at the event ignored my suggestion as ridiculous and went on their habitual way, but many stopped me in the hallways, coffee shop, or elevator and told me that all the usual conference frenzy had shifted and the way they were paying attention to others had changed. Several people mentioned that they also felt more confidence and connection, speaking when they assumed others might be paying attention to them in this graceful way. If there can be heaven on earth, why not angels on earth — angels going around illuminating another's spot of grace?

Whom or What Are You Serving?

Love is that condition in the human spirit so profound that it empowers us to develop courage; to trust that courage, and build bridges with it; to trust those bridges, and cross over them so we can attempt to reach each other.

MAYA ANGELOU, *Even the Stars Look Lonesome*

Join the revolution of secret angels. Who says you need feathers? I want every child born into this world to be blessed, as I was, by someone who could see his or her uniqueness. I want every person alive to remember the legacy of dreams, prayers, sweat, and hard-earned wisdom running through the river of our blood.

Poet and theologian John O'Donohue defines soul as the place where the intimate and the infinite meet. I believe my grandmother would say this is the exact location of the spot of grace. In my experience, it is also the place that seeds our greatest potential for influence.

Influence is an equal-opportunity employer. Unlimited amounts are available to each of us. As I wrote in the last section, a teenager named Jerome in a migrant labor camp in Florida changed forever the way I think about learning and difference. He inspired me to write three books that tens of thousands of people have read. Who knows how many children were ultimately influenced by Jerome's effect on me?

The people mentioned in this book have influenced hundreds of thousands of lives without even knowing it. All it took was a simple act of recognition that changed everything for one person, who then went on to make a difference for thousands of others.

Life gives us seeds as a way of saying, "Please."

The gifts you carry, even if you do not know what they are or have not felt them stirring in you for decades, are needed by the rest of us. Your spot of grace means that you do belong. If you allow yourself to know this, you will also come to recognize that in every person you meet, there is a seed of light. *All* those gifts are needed now. Each and every one of us belongs. There can be no orphans; there can be no exiles or aliens.

Only when we appreciate the unique gifts that each of us has to offer and the shining web of connection that holds us all can we open ourselves to the full potential of what we can achieve together.

Prove you do make a difference and help this spark take hold. Send me stories of how others have helped you recognize your spot of grace and of the epiphanies you have created for them. Risk the reach. Do it as a way of loving the life you live. Let the stories begin to pour out like a river. Stand on its banks, and notice what we can truly make possible.

This is the way you can spread the flow of grace into the world: send your imperfectly perfect stories to www.dawnamarkova.com.

Have some friends over for a party and encourage them to write and tell each other their stories. How about the kids you know? Encourage them, collect their stories, send them to the website so we can create a Kid's Spot of Grace book. Do you know or work with elders? Are *you* an elder? Cultivating wisdom is our job. Collect and send in your stories. It's a way we can all grandparent grace into the future.

orchard

acknowledgments

Blessed is the influence of one true, loving, human soul on another.

GEORGE ELIOT

One Sunday while my grandmother was brushing her silky white hair, I ran my fingers over the carvings on top of the small camphorwood box that sat on her dresser. She put the brush down and placed the box in her own palm, opening and closing it several times. Then she said softly, "Hands, hearts, minds, boxes — they can all be opened or closed. They're all capable of both, yes?" I nodded, and she stretched the box out to me.

To write this book, I've opened my heart, hands, and mind to release some of the seeds from that box. Every time I attempt to write this last page, I water those seeds with my tears. I strain between feeling an abundance of gratitude for all I have been given and the hopeless inadequacy of ever truly expressing it all.

If you look deeply on the pages of this book, you will not only find the stories of over a hundred loving, human souls who took the time and reached out to answer the call; you will also find the fingerprints of those who inspired them and made it possible to write the stories in the first place.

Appreciations to:

The ultimate gardener: Mary Jane Ryan

The branches: Andy Bryner

The ones who make it all matter: David Peck and Angie McArthur

The angel: Joan M. Sapiro

The caretaker: Georgia Hughes

The garden devas at New World Library: Kristen Cashman, Mary Ann Casler, Munro Magruder, Monique Muhlenkamp, Tona Pearce Myers, and Jonathan Wichmann

The roots: Rachel Bagby, Sylvia and Seymour Boorstein, Milton Erickson, MD, Sensei Richard Kuboyama, Joanna Macy, Sensei Lloyd Miyashiro, Mark Nepo, Parker Palmer, Debra Chamberlin Taylor, Jai Uttal, and Julie Wester

The ones who did the heavy lifting: Kay Brouillette, Jim and Nanci Sapiro, Lewis Sapiro, and Tom and Teri Sapiro

Joan's angels: Christina, Ann Hayes, Kathy, Nicki, and the Denver Hospice

My angels: Simone Amber, Kenny Ausabel and Nina Simons, Patrick Burke, Rachel and Bill Edwards, Peris Gumz, Julia Johnston, Karen Koshgarian, Don McIlraith, Ana Li McIlraith, Betsy McKinney, Anne Powell, Linda Ruth, Barbara and Michael Streibel, Frieda Todd, Michael and Justine Toms, and Conna Lee Weinberg

The ones who sat in audiences and circles with me, living inside of questions that only their souls could answer.

And you, dear reader, who have accompanied me with such kind attention through all the days and nights that this seed has been growing.

about the author

Dawna Markova, PhD, is internationally known for her ground-breaking research in the fields of learning and perception. She is the CEO of Professional Thinking Partners and a research member of the Society for Organizational Learning. In 2003, Dawna cofounded SmartWired.org, an organization devoted to maximizing individual and collective human potential in all areas of life.

As one of the editors of the Random Acts of Kindness series, she was influential in launching a national movement to help counter America's crisis of violence. She is the author of *I Will Not Die an Unlived Life*, *The SMART Parenting Revolution*, *The Open Mind* book and audio series, *No Enemies Within*, *How Your Child IS Smart*, and *Learning Unlimited*.

Dawna was recently honored with the Visions to Action Award "for people who have made a profound contribution to the world." A long-term cancer survivor (she was told she had six months to live almost thirty years ago), Dawna has appeared on numerous television programs and is a frequent guest on National Public Radio and New Dimensions Media. At business and educational conferences around the globe, she has inspired audiences to live with purpose and passion.

To find out about Dawna's upcoming inspirational speeches and training on realizing purpose and passion, visit www.dawnamarkova.com. To learn more about her work recognizing, utilizing, and developing intellectual capital in organizations, visit www.ptpinc.org.